Routledge Revivals

Europe and the Turks

Europe and the Turks

Noel Buxton

Routledge
Taylor & Francis Group
Routledge Revivals

First published in 1907 by Methuen & Co. Ltd

This edition first published in 2019 by Routledge
2 Park Square, Milton Park, Abingdon, Oxon, OX14 4RN
and by Routledge
52 Vanderbilt Avenue, New York, NY 10017, USA

Routledge is an imprint of the Taylor & Francis Group, an informa business

Publisher's Note

The publisher has gone to great lengths to ensure the quality of this reprint but points out that some imperfections in the original copies may be apparent.

Disclaimer

The publisher has made every effort to trace copyright holders and welcomes correspondence from those they have been unable to contact.

A Library of Congress record exists under ISBN:

ISBN 13: 978-0-367-19935-7 (hbk)
ISBN 13: 978-0-367-19936-4 (pbk)
ISBN 13: 978-0-429-24425-4 (ebk)

EUROPE AND THE TURKS

AUSTRIA-HUNGARY
RUMANIA
BULGARIA
SERVIA
TURKEY
ASIA MINOR
BLACK SEA
Sea of Azof
Crimea
ADRIATIC SEA
ITALY
Ionian Sea
MEDITERRANEAN SEA
Sicily
Crete
Cyprus
Bosnia
Montenegro
Macedonia
CONSTANTINOPLE
BUCHAREST
Adrianople
Philippopolis
Sofia
Belgrade
Odessa
Kherson
Sevastopol
Athens
Smyrna
Salonica
Rhodes
Malta (Br.)
Valetta
Messina
Catania
Taranto
Brindisi
Bari
Ancona
Agram
Trieste
Szegedin
Temesvar
Varna
Burgas
Galatz
Braila
Constantza
Rustchuk
Plevna
Shumla
Nish
Uskub
Monastir
Valona
Corfu
Patras
Zante
Kalamata
C. Matapan
Cerigo
Milos
Candia
Gallipoli
Brusa
Ismid
Scutari
Angora
Konia
Adana
Mersina
Alexandretta
Aleppo
Kaisaria
Sinope
Samsun
Kastamuni
Amasia
Tokat
Aidin
Manissa
Larissa
Trikala
Arta
Tripolitza
Jassy
20
30
40
C. to B. 582
C. to N. 456
C. to R. 620
C. to O. 344
Naples to P. Said 1113
Malta to Constantinople 847
Malta to P. Said
Brindisi to P. Said

EUROPE AND THE TURKS

BY

NOEL BUXTON, M.P.

WITH MAPS

METHUEN & CO. LTD.
36 ESSEX STREET W.C.
LONDON

Originally Published by Mr. John Murray in 1907
First Published by Methuen & Co. Ltd.
Second Edition (Revised with new matter), in 1912

TO

C. F. G. MASTERMAN

M.P.

MY COMPANION IN

MACEDONIA

PREFACE

A CONFLICT between Turkey and European States is a fundamental one. Other animosities are the result of sentiments which may yield to reason; this is the adjustment of boundaries wrongly placed, the inevitable clash of order and progress with fatalism and ascendancy. Every other conflict might yield to the spread of education; but, short of a miracle, the present war was inevitable.

It was long foretold by all who knew the Balkans at first hand. Three solutions alone could have averted it: reform from within, reform by suasion, and reform by coercion. This volume depicts the futilities of the first. "Young Turkey" (and it is not without keen regret that I embrace an alternative distasteful to the few Turkish genuine reformers) has shattered the last hopes of reform from the second. Divisions and egoism among the Powers has too long delayed the third. There is no course left but war.

To trace its cause is not useless, if it enables us to grasp the conditions of settlement which can alone remove what Lord Lansdowne described as a standing menace to European peace.

I wish to express my gratitude to Mr. J. H. Whitehouse, M.P., for his help in reading and correcting the proofs.

NOEL BUXTON

2, PRINCE'S GATE, S.W.

CONTENTS

APPENDICES

MAPS

ILLUSTRATION

S.E. EUROPE IN 16TH & 17TH CENTURIES.
BOHEMIA
HUNGARY
AUSTRIA
IMPERIAL
SIEBENBURGEN
MOLDAVIA
JEDISAN
TURKISH HUNGARY
WALLACHIA
DANUBE
TURKISH EMPIRE

S.E. EUROPE A.D. 1812.
AUSTRIAN EMPIRE
HUNGARY
R. PRUTH
DANUBE
BOSNIA
SERVIA
TURKISH EMPIRE

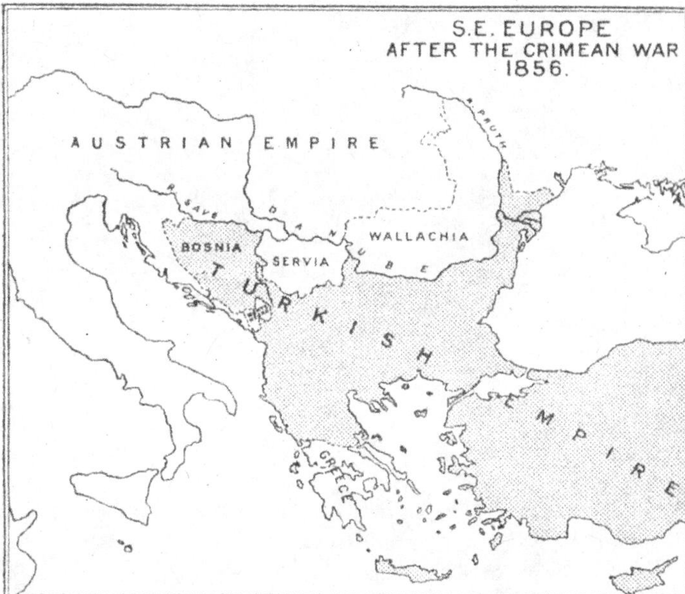
S.E. EUROPE
AFTER THE CRIMEAN WAR
1856.
AUSTRIAN EMPIRE
R. PRUTH
R. SAVE
DANUBE
WALLACHIA
BOSNIA
SERVIA
TURKISH EMPIRE
GREECE

S.E.EUROPE
SAN STEFANO TREATY
1878.
AUSTRIA – HUNGARY
R. PRUTH
R. SAVE
DANUBE
RUMANIA
BOSNIA
SERVIA
MONTE NEGRO
BULGARIA
GREECE

EUROPE AND THE TURKS

CHAPTER I

THE PAST

The battle of East and West—The cradle of Christendom—The Moslem invasion—The West preserved—Europe in danger—Pitt and Burke—English intervention—Liberation—The Crimea—1876—The Berlin Congress—The wrong horse—Rebellion

TO-DAY we are witnessing a further phase of the battle between the East and the West.

If the history of Christendom had not been omitted from our education, the Near East would recall memories of the earlier struggles between barbarism and civilization. Here was founded that system of established Christian government to which, for good or for evil, we owe our very existence. Here Constantine, the first Christian Emperor, having established the capital of the Roman Empire at the gateway of Europe and Asia, declared Christianity the State religion. Here he founded three churches, that we may still visit to-day, dedicating them (in a spirit of compromise with the old philosophy) to Wisdom, Peace, and Resurrection; and in them was celebrated the Christian Sacrament, which remained in unbroken continuity for 1,100 years. The Church of San Sofia, until the year 1453, though the Pope of Rome had withdrawn from his allegiance, could claim to be the headquarters of the Christian world. Constantinople was at once the centre and the outpost of Christendom, for it was not many generations after Constantine that Mohammed founded his warlike Church, and already—700 years after Christ—the Saracens threatened the Empire. Meanwhile the savage tribes from the North had invaded the Eastern no less than the Western Empire. Slavs and Bulgarians, a tribe akin to the Turk, drove the Greek element southward. It was not long before the Greek monks Cyril and Methodios converted the Slavs to the gentler faith. They first invented the Cyrillic alphabet still used by the Slav races, while Methodios impressed the message of Christianity upon his savage hearers by the use of pictures, so, perhaps, originating the passionate devotion to icons which may be seen to-day in any Orthodox church. Here was the greatest missionary achievement of Eastern Christianity. But the possession of a common faith did not in the East, any more than in the West, inspire political unity. First the Bulgarian and then the Servian Czars drove back the Greeks to the confines of Byzantium. The feud of Slav and

Greek was further complicated by the religious enmity of East and West, and by the rise of Protestant sects like the Bogomils, who, especially in Bosnia, kept their rulers busy with the task of persecution. The Turk was not slow to profit by such an opportunity. Where now the American Protestant College overlooks the loveliest views of the Bosphorus the Sultan crossed into Europe. The East too late appealed for help to the West. The Pope hesitated, and in 1389 the Servian Empire, which then ruled the Balkan Peninsula, was destroyed at the great battle of Kossovo. Whole populations were butchered or compelled to adopt Islam, and Constantinople, which had been isolated until it should fall an easy prey, was taken in 1453. Mohammedan tyranny overwhelmed like a flood some of the richest countries of Europe, and thus were sacrificed, not only the Byzantine Empire and the Slavonic peoples, but also Hungary and Southern Russia, till only some 200 years ago the alien had penetrated the very centre of Europe and besieged Vienna.[1] We forget how short a time has passed since, with vivid realism, men repeated the Psalm, "The heathen have come into Thy inheritance; Thy holy places have they defiled."

Many a stately ruin still shows the traveller in Turkey what the East suffered to save the West. Modern education leaves us totally ignorant of our debt to the Eastern Christian. Romish contempt

[1] See map.

of the Orthodox Church is, oddly enough, retained by Protestants. We ignore the culture that she developed, her splendid evangelism, and the protection she gave to the West. We forget that before the Turk came she was leading the world in civilization. Such is our prejudice and ignorance that the relics of her arts, which in rare cases remote monasteries have saved from the deliberate vandalism of the invader, strike us with surprise. Greek, Serb, Bulgar, Roumanian, Croat, Albanian, Russian, Hungarian—all these suffered in holding back the tide of destruction from the rest of Europe. Alien and barbarous ideals, disgusting and demoralizing to the Christian, were imposed upon many nations, and over a great part of Europe still hold sway. As Mr. Gladstone said, the Christian who retained his faith at the price of slavery, when by recanting he could obtain every favour, is entitled to the name of martyr, and to him Europe owes the gratitude that is due to the rampart which saved it.

Liberty is coming back by degrees, but progress is slow, and the Government which has in fact, though not in intention, done most to impede liberation is our own. For the salient fact in the modern history of the Near East is the intervention of England as the saviour of Turkey. This is the astonishing fact which to the present generation is hardly known, and which contradicts our great traditions. But for this our responsibility would be no greater than that of the other European States, and could be discharged, perhaps, by leaving the matter to the Powers more closely concerned by local proximity.

The history of our relations with Turkey is a curious one ; foreigners call it typically British. Up to the end of the seventeenth century hatred of the Turk was universal in Europe. Catholic and Protestant States alike were in danger of losing their very existence, and though Protestants were to be found who welcomed the Turk as a scourge to the Catholic, the common peril brought all together when the Turk, in 1683, laid siege to Vienna.[1] As late as 1701, in "The Turkish History" of Sir Paul Rycaut, the diplomatist, we read of "the Turks who are grown formidable to all the world." Even England, though beyond the seas, shared the danger and the sense of horror which Turkish enormities inspired. All Western Europe had joined in the Crusades, and the sense of unity,

[1] The summons delivered to the besieged ran as follows : "The most happy, invincible, and mighty Emperor of the Universe, the Image of God living on the Earth, who is by a multitude of miracles become the greatest Sovereign of both one and the other world, hath sent his armies without number, that they should take Vienna, and there establish the worship of our religion, and we exhort you before we unsheath our terrible scimitars to embrace our holy religion. But in case you are obstinate, we will put all to the sword as is commanded by our Holy Law."

inherited from Charlemagne and the Holy Roman Empire, had not expired; not even the Reformation had entirely killed it. At the end of the eighteenth century, though ten generations had lived and died since the great cleavage of Christendom, Pitt's proposal that England should join with Turkey against the encroachments of Russia was received with such hostility by Fox and Lord Grey that the Minister, though at the height of his power, was compelled to abandon it. To side with the Turk was treason to the highest law, and the general sentiment was voiced by Burke when he declared that "any Christian Power was to be preferred to these destructive savages."

Yet within a very few years the outlook was entirely changed. The Turk had ceased to conquer, and commerce became the supreme interest. For England in particular the trade with India had grown to be a matter of vital concern, and men suddenly found that their duty to Europe might endanger their profits. The righteous indignation which had met Pitt's proposal had died away, and for a hundred years financial interest struggled successfully with justice for the control of our policy. Political ideals had sunk from the conception of Christendom to that of the balance of power, and we used the Turk to check the growing influence of Russia. To save Turkey we fought one great war and prepared for another. It is a strange paradox that during this same hundred years we gained a name for befriending freedom, and that, too, on the very field—the soil of the Turkish Empire—where England was opposing it. For though this reputation is mainly due to the work of Palmerston, Russell, and Gladstone in the liberation of Italy, yet it began with Canning and with the fame of Byron as a fellow-soldier with the Greeks, and it was maintained by Gladstone's stupendous effort to checkmate the policy of Disraeli. Every Harrow boy is nurtured on the song that tells how

> "Byron lay, Byron lay,
> Dying for freedom, far away";

while Gladstone's gift of the Ionian Islands to Greece and his classic denunciation of Turkey are perhaps the most memorable, because the most unique, features of his life.

And although we did our best for Turkey, yet liberation proceeded all through the century. Greeks, Serbs, Roumanians, all rebelled. Europe, tired of the long distraction of the Greek War of Liberation, combined in 1827 to sink the Turkish fleet at Navarino, and though the temper of certain classes in England was clearly shown in Wellington's description of this achievement as an "untoward event," the independence of Hellas was accomplished for ever. Servia and Roumania won the elements of freedom by their own heroic courage, and it was a reckless bravery, so well described in the brilliant pages of Mr. Benson's "Vintage," that liberated Greece.

Then came the advance of Russia, the pathetic hesitation of Lord Aberdeen's Cabinet between concern for the Eastern Christians on the one hand and national alarms on the other, drifting finally to the Crimean War. In all the literature of the Turkish question there is none more interesting than the Duke of Argyll's pamphlet on "Our Responsibility for Turkey," where, writing in 1895, he defends the principle on which he and Mr. Gladstone, the last survivors of the Aberdeen Cabinet, supported the cause of war. In the Treaty of Paris which followed the war we find declarations in favour of equal rights between Christians and Mohammedan—a sop to the British conscience. These the Turks were wise enough to embody in the formal proclamation known as the Hatti-Humayun of 1856, which has ever since been a dead letter. Lord Aberdeen did something to relieve his sense of regret by urgent dispatches to the Sublime Porte, of which the following is an example of special interest:—

"The Christian Powers . . . will now require from the Porte due consideration for their feelings as members of a religious community, and interested as such in the fate of all who, notwithstanding shades of difference, unite in a common belief in the essential doctrines of Christianity; and they will not endure that the Porte shall insult and trample on their faith by treating as a criminal any person who embraces it."

Russia, foiled in the frontal attack, turned to more diplomatic methods. Hardly had the British ships returned from the Bosphorus than the Slavonic people of European Turkey, disappointed for the first but not the last time, began to cast about for means of attracting other help. Adventurous spirits conceived the idea that, if Russia were not allowed to help them, some effective sympathy might be won by appealing to the West as fellow Roman Catholics. The Pope was asked to recognize congregations of Orthodox Christians, though still retaining their married priesthood and liturgy in their own language, as belonging to the Roman Church. This Uniate community, as it was named, began to grow apace; but Russia took alarm and offered a more enticing bait. She supported the revival of the old Bulgarian Church, and this proved a stronger attraction. The Southern Slavs had long been exploited and denationalized by the clergy of the Greek Patriarchate. They were not allowed their own language, and their books were destroyed; they had learned to call themselves Greeks, so that Kinglake, when writing "Eöthen," did not even mention the existence of Bulgars. The new *Exarchate*, as it was called, met the desire for a revived national existence. Within ten years the once downtrodden spirit of the Bulgar peasants was equal to rebellious efforts. Rifles were smuggled in, cannons were secretly made out of cherry-trees, and in 1875 the insurrection described by Mr. Vazof in "Under the Yoke" took place. This was savagely repressed, and in the following year the indignation of England was suddenly roused by "the Bulgarian atrocities." The people of the little town of Batak, attacked by Turks, had taken refuge within the church, and there been butchered, down to the smallest child. The church to this day is filled with their bones, while a new one has been erected to the memory of Lady Strangford, who, with other English people, carried relief to the neighbouring villages.

Parliament was still sitting when undeniable evidence arrived from the correspondent of the *Daily News*, Mr. Edwin Pears, now leader of the Consular Bar at Constantinople, who took the risk of visiting Batak. Mr. Gladstone, through his pamphlet, "Bulgarian Atrocities," revealed the ghastly facts and demanded a reforming policy. But the Government had a large majority, and scoffed at sentiment. The imposition of serious reforms was prevented by England's influence. Russia went to war. Plevna was at last captured, and, at the cost of 10,000 lives, the rampart of the Balkan range was scaled at the Shipka Pass. In March, 1878, the Russians were at San Stefano within sight of Constantinople, and the famous treaty was passed by which practically the whole of European Turkey, with the exception of

Albania, became the free principality of Bulgaria. Every district where bloodshed has since occurred was freed by this compact.[1]

But England would have no dangerous liberations. The Prime Minister had rightly gauged the English capacity for panic. He talked of protecting the Christians by a system of military Consuls, who should practically dominate the Turkish Administration, and all that Mr. Gladstone's eloquence could do was to induce some ninety Liberals to vote against the preparations for war with Russia. Lord Randolph Churchill tried hard to change his leader's determination, but national pride and fear possessed the governing classes like a fever. One of our most prominent admirals remembers how when the news of San Stefano arrived, he was attending Queen Victoria upon the royal yacht. He recalls the simple determination with which the Queen, on hearing how the Czar's troops were on the Sea of Marmora, accurately voicing the national mood, remarked, "They must go out." There was no question of refusing our demand, for the Russians were receiving their supplies by sea.

The Congress of Berlin was called. The English Premier (though he could not speak French) bluffed the Powers with consummate skill. Cyprus was secretly granted us by treaty in return for our promise to protect Turkey by force, and 5,000

[1] See map.

villages which had found themselves actually released were put back under the regime of murder and rapine.

Had it not been for Mr. Gladstone the effect of the Russo-Turkish War would have been nothing more than the annexation of Bosnia by Austro-Hungary. As it was, while Macedonia was lost to the Turks, a part of Bulgaria was freed and Servia enlarged. Mr. Disraeli concealed his regret at this mutilation of the Turkish Empire by claiming that he had achieved its "consolidation."

When the Russophobe fever had subsided Mr. Gladstone aroused the country to its senses, appealing, not only to humanity, but to an intelligent view of national interests, urging that a barrier against Russia would be found, not in a dying despotism, but in the breasts of free men. The election of 1880 showed how a Jingo policy had misrepresented the nation, but it was too late; the Turkish question was no longer upon the table, and all that Mr. Gladstone could do was to persuade the Powers to join in demanding the execution of some minor provisions of the Berlin Treaty. Sir Henry Layard was recalled from Constantinople as being unqualified to express the Liberal policy. Mr. Goschen, who took his place, proved a successful instrument in persuading the youthful Sultan, who relinquished Thessaly on the mere proposal of Mr. Gladstone to effect an occupation of Smyrna. The Berlin Treaty by

Article 23 promised autonomous government to Macedonia. It is thus to the public law of Europe that she appeals. All that was actually achieved was the addition of a few square miles to Montenegro and the annexation of Thessaly to Greece. The Government of 1880 was soon immersed in Irish and Egyptian troubles. Lord Edmond Fitzmaurice was sent as Commissioner to devise reforms, but his scheme was never enforced, and Macedonia was forgotten.

No one now denies that our conduct at this crisis sacrificed, in actual fact, some millions of European villagers to pain and degradation for our ends ; but this result has been somewhat obscured by the sense that it was also futile for ourselves. We would gladly forget it. Yet even self-interest forbids us to let the question alone, while the most elementary sense of honour demands that we shall spare no single effort to redeem the victims of our action.

In 1878 the turning-point in Near Eastern history had, though unexpected, arrived, and in six years the policy of supporting the Turk was admitted to have been a mistake, even more completely than after the Crimean War. For one thing at least had been accomplished—the Bulgarian race had gained a footing in the world ; the leading figure in the Balkan drama had appeared upon the stage. Russia had created Bulgaria, and we had regarded her as a Russian outpost; but almost immediately it appeared that both we and the Russians had been in the wrong, for Bulgaria proved a refractory child, and when she was attacked by Servia, Russia took revenge by suddenly withdrawing all the 300 officers whom she had supplied to the new State. Bulgaria's army was left with no leader of more than company rank. Among these captains and lieutenants, however, were men of genius, and by an extraordinary *tour de force* Bulgaria won. Russia was angry, and Bulgaria turned for help to Russia's foe. England also had quickly found that she, in Lord Salisbury's phrase, had "put her money on the wrong horse," for Turkey fell quickly under Russian influence, and when, in 1884, the two parts of Bulgaria, which England in 1878 stipulated should be kept asunder, declared themselves one it was the British Ambassador who saved the Bulgarian State from Turkish and Russian vengeance. Russia called a conference of Ambassadors, and proposed that the Turk should be empowered to reoccupy Eastern Roumelia—that is, the southern half of Bulgaria. Most of the Powers were with her. Here was a chance for a vigorous man. There are those who well remember how our Ambassador, Sir William White, first exhausted the conference by thundering declamations through the whole of a hot afternoon at Tophane, then obtained the adjournment of the meeting, and afterwards contrived to prevent another being called—so soon had Mr.

Gladstone's prophecy come true, that if we wanted a bulwark against Russia, we must liberate the nations of European Turkey. Had we done so, greater Bulgaria might to-day be strong enough to obviate any further question of the disposal of European Turkey. Dishonesty was the wrong policy, and the mistake has still to be redeemed.

Doubtless the action that proved so regrettable, and which led to the re-enslavement of the people of Macedonia, was adopted without realizing its enormity. It proved also the greatest folly, though by an inscrutable destiny the chief sufferers have been, not the wrongdoer but the wronged. Since 1878 the demoralization of the Turk, once trusted to resist Russia, has proceeded apace, and disorder has, by general consent, become even more intolerable than in the old days.

The people of Macedonia, abandoned by the Powers, were compelled to take the sword themselves, and in spite of the efforts of the Powers to restrain them, some progress has been made since the Berlin Treaty.

Rebellious movements elsewhere have incited them. First the Armenians, who since the insurrection of the Greeks had been employed as the brains of the Empire, misjudged the humanity of Europe, and put all to the risk in 1894. The degradation of Christendom had not been realized by any section of mankind. The Sultan himself was astonished to find that his deliberate butcheries went unpunished; he became bolder still, and drove home the lesson he desired to teach by killing 6,000 Armenians before the windows of the foreign embassies. It was the turn of the Powers themselves to be astonished, but it was their own indifference which had made it possible to complete in this way their ignominy. The sacrifice produced no visible gain, and Armenia remains where she was.

The incredible risks of insurrection are incurred, because when the choice is between a life of continual outrage against every feeling held most dear on the one hand, and on the other hand the danger of death, the latter is the lesser evil.

Greece has been more successful, for by risking the displeasure of the Powers and the humiliation of an unsuccessful war, she has obtained the liberation of the Greeks of Crete.

Macedonia has not been so fortunate. For fifteen years the spirit of the Macedonians appeared to be crushed by disappointment, but then began to appear the germ of an organization which has proved itself one of the most remarkable in the history of revolutions. In 1899 the Internal Committee, as it is called, had done nothing bigger than the capture of one small Turkish picket and some acts of revenge upon specially obnoxious Turks; but it had issued appeals to Europe, and collected rifles in Macedonia, while, owing to the outrages inflicted on villages suspected of concealing arms, Sir Philip Currie had sent a diplomat to the interior for the purpose of inquiring into the grievances of the peasants, thus calling the attention of Europe. In 1902 dissensions in the Committee led to an abortive rising. The rising was followed by such widespread cruelty that some thousand of refugees, abandoning all that they had, fled through the mountains and forests into Bulgaria, where, at the romantic monastery of Rilo, Europeans helped to relieve them. The credit of informing the world that the Turk was again beginning his bloody work once more fell to the *Daily News*, whose special correspondent undertook an adventurous ride in that winter. The rapid increase of disorder compelled the Powers to exchange views, and in February, 1903, the two Eastern Empires, fearing an encroachment by the small Powers on the field which they had decided to occupy, issued the so-called Vienna Scheme of reform. The Turk accepted it at once, so mild were its proposals, and things went on as before. But the danger had roused the Turk to the only method of keeping order which his intellect could understand, and in July the rebels found that, owing to the untimely haste of their more reckless spirits and the brutal suppression which ensued, they were driven to serious insurrection. Over 100 villages were burned, and 3,000 peasants killed. Sixty thousand were made homeless. British charity, backed by Lord Lansdowne, alone prevented their destruction by cold and hunger.

England suggested a Christian Governor, but Russia and Austria, by the Murszteg Scheme of October, 1903, again endeavoured to keep the field to themselves, while leaving the country in such disorder that they could intervene more successfully for their interests at a suitable time. But Lord Lansdowne pushed them forward farther than they desired, and the other Powers obtained a footing in the matter by the provision that officers of all the five Governments should be allotted spheres of influence in which to supervise the gendarmerie. His proposal, however, for European control was rejected. After long discussions and the acceptance of Turkish commissions, the officers took up their residence (no powers were assigned to them) in April, 1904. So little had they effected by the following winter that Lord Lansdowne again proposed an advance, urging that a Commission of the Powers should be established, with actual control of the administration.[1] But the susceptibilities of Russia and Austria once more prevented the respective Cabinets of France and Italy from giving their support, and in the end, though Lord Lansdowne's effort culminated in the occupation of Mitylene by the international fleet in December,

[1] See Appendix.

1905, no real control was obtained. Nothing more, in fact, resulted than the recognition that the matter was one for the whole Concert, and the appointment of Commissioners from each Power to "supervise" the financial side of the Macedonian government. The machinery of reform was established, but there was as yet no steam in the shape of executive authority to drive it.

Things drifted from bad to worse. The toll of deaths by violence passed 200 a month. Some of the European officers resigned their posts in disgust with the nature of their task, which, they complained, was limited to compiling butchers' bills! Clerks in the British Embassy at Pera found their time filled with the copying of these gruesome statistics. Sir Edward Grey appeared less active than Lord Lansdowne, and addressing a deputation in July, 1907, declared that nothing could be done.

But things took an unexpected turn in 1908, when the Austrian Foreign Minister, Baron von Aehrenthal, achieved an agreement with Turkey for the right to build further railways in the Sanjak of Novi Bazar. Sir Edward Grey seized the opportunity. He announced to a surprised House of Commons that the British Government proposed a Viceroy of Macedonia responsible, not to the Sultan but to the Powers. England took her true place as leader responsible for the past, and therefore responsible for making proposals.

For the first time we had Russia as a friend. The means of forcing the scheme on Turkey were to be discussed with Russian Ministers, when King Edward met the Czar at Reval. The "Reval Programme," implying the new factor of Anglo-Russian action, convinced intelligent Turkey that at last the Powers might act. The Young Turks, to save their country's honour, took their lives in their hands. The "bloodless revolution" was accomplished; rebel prisoners were set free; harmony between Turk and Christian made intervention from without absurd.

The Reval Programme was dropped. Even the officers, whose supervision influenced the course of events, in spite of protests from such observers as the Balkan Committee, were withdrawn. The Young Turks were given a free hand. Even those most sceptical of their powers had to face the fact that assistance must now be sought, not from the Powers but from the Turkish reformers themselves. Bulgaria, ready to seize the chance of attacking Turkey, was restrained by the united opinions of friends and critics alike. The possibility of a reformed Turkey appealed to all believers in nationality, for the most part identified with advocates of reform on grounds of humanity. The heroism of the rebel Turks, their self-effacement, and consummate efficiency, compelled admiration even in those most doubtful of their political morals. But the obvious danger of failure, through Jingoism in their own traditions, and the bigotry of the uneducated mass, dictated rather active sympathy than cold criticism, on the part of those who could give them prestige, lend them experts, and influence their views. Accordingly, when England, who, from her hostility to Abdul Hamid, was the idol of Young Turkey, repelled their advances and befriended their Old Turk enemies, German influence revived. Baron von Mareschall seized the much-needed opportunity to recover influence. The German element, which thus gained the upper hand, was naturally militarist. The spirit of ascendancy triumphed. The local claims of the Yemen, Macedonia, and Albania were answered by "Turkification." Continental ideals of exact uniformity and absolute centralization prevailed against the primary need for personal security, equal justice, and education.

But if England and Germany had worked together reform might have come quickly enough to remove the excuse of the Balkan States for war. But in any case the hope was a forlorn one. English observers endeavoured through personal acquaintance with Turkish leaders to make their strong desire for British support a lever towards reform. Considerable progress was indeed made towards efficiency in the army, the Treasury, the Customs, and public works.

But the punishment of Moslems for crimes against Christians remained the rock on which progress foundered. The criticisms of British sympathizers grew stronger with the lapse of time which justified them. Finally, in 1912, the appointment ot Europeans to executive authority was suggested as the only way to avert a revival of the Reval policy of intervention by the Powers. The suggestion was adopted. But in the summer the ugly fact of massacre had once more to be faced. Meanwhile the small States and their nationals in Turkey, driven together by the pressure of a Government more active or more centralizing than of old, had accomplished the miracle of co-operation. Faced even with the danger of war, Turkey gave a final proof of unwillingness to meet the standards of European civilization. When Bulgaria had already mobilized, Turkish meetings were protesting against the hanging of a single Moslem for the butchery of Christians at Kotchana. "Reform from within" was past praying for. The divisions of the Powers, their indifference to reform, whether by aiding Turkey or coercing her, the chauvinism of her rulers, above all, the bigoted ignorance of her people, had left but one solution available—reform from without, and reform by force.

In default of a leader sufficiently active to carry the Concert forward across the bridge which lies between "supervision" and "control," it awaited the solution which diplomats profess to avoid—the solution by war.

CHAPTER II

FACTORS IN THE PROBLEM

Complications—Rise of Nationalism—Slav *v.* Greek—Rival claims—The Great Powers to blame—Russia checked by England—Austrian and German ambition—France and Italy indifferent—England uncertain—Need of a leader

SOME of the richest parts of the globe are lying wasted under the Turkish yoke, but the world is sick of the question, and it is almost with pleasure that the politician arrives at sufficient knowledge of the matter to be able to say that it is too complicated for solution. No doubt the difficulties are great: what great reform was ever easy? To-day the abolition of slavery passes for an obvious mark of a civilized State, but it required a Parliamentary campaign of thirty years to bring it to an end, and that, too, within the last century.

So long as a Great Power held the frontier of Europe, the progress of liberation was rapid. When, in 1683, the Turkish armies failed to take Vienna, the tide of Islam had reached its high-water mark.

Austria began to recover lost ground, and by the end of the eighteenth century her fortresses were established along the whole line, from east to west, of the Danube and the Save.[1] In a single century she had driven the Turk back into the Balkans, and the danger which in our great-grandfathers' time men well remembered as threatening to extinguish Europe was passed. The subject peoples of the Turkish Empire themselves began to take courage, and early in the nineteenth century the Greek, the Serb, and the Roumanian began to throw off the yoke. National feeling made the burden intolerable. When these little States had been established, the Turk was no longer face to face with a Power stronger than himself, but with feeble nations unable to make headway against him. Thus, in order to carry forward the flag of civilization, it was necessary that these little Powers should work together. Formerly the subjects of the Sultan saw themselves liberated by great armies, which marched across their lands. Happy it was for those who, like the Hungarians, obtained their liberty first, and found their national existence afterwards. A harder fate attends the Southern Slav and the Greek, who are unable to drive back the Turk without the closest military co-operation, yet are debarred from such union by the confusion of claims to the still unliberated country.

[1] See Maps.

Even so the neighbouring Great Powers, Russia and Austria, would have continued the strife had they not been hampered by the growth of rivalry in the larger world of the European Concert. The Great Powers obey no law; each bows to no higher court of arbitration than the ability of the others to stand in his way. Some of them sit round the death-bed of the Turkish Empire like the settlers round an Indian reserve in America, ready to rush in when the native rights are brought to an end. Here, and not in the feuds of the local nations, now resolutely composed, lies the real difficulty of liberating Macedonia.

The rival claims of the small Powers have a natural and solid basis. Extreme danger has overridden them, but they are worth noting.

What is the essential cleavage in the Balkans? It is that the Slav and Greek overlap each other in such a way that any possible frontier between the two must hand over considerable populations to an alien Government. As if Providence had not done enough by this overlapping in the way of complication, the Powers increased it by creating the principality of Bulgaria, thus dividing the Slav element into two nations, when it might have been one. There are, therefore, three chief claimants to Macedonia, each demanding, after the fashion in vogue in an Eastern bazaar, at least double what it would take. All three base their claim on history and race, the Serb and the Bulgarian also on language. The

Bulgarian further insists that a man's nationality—which in this part of the world is synonymous with Churchmanship—may be known by the Church he actually belongs to. The Greek, in mediaeval style, prefers as an index the Church he ought not to have abandoned. You may award the verdict according as you think that history, blood, language or religion should be the basis of States.

The Chauvinist of each nation puts his case wildly, and for our purpose it is better to imagine what a delegate from each nation would say if empowered to state his claim at the Hague Conference. The essential facts could be stated as follows :—

The Greek.—"My claim to Macedonia comes down from antiquity. We are the heirs of Alexander the Great. The Byzantine Empire, at all events, was Greek. For seven centuries we fought the Mohammedan, and saved Europe from destruction. We, too, were the first to set ourselves free. Byron and Gladstone were on our side. We gave culture to the world, and to this day we are the civilizing element in the Near East. Till the last half-century all the Christians in Macedonia acknowledged the Patriarch of the Greek Church, and called themselves Greeks. Give us, at all events, the whole of Southern Macedonia and Thrace, for their people are Greek."

The Greek has long supplied the brain of the East. Egypt herself can hardly be governed, much less grow rich, without the Greeks, and there are parts of

Macedonia which it would be cruel not to add to the dominions of King George.

The Serb.—"We also ruled the whole peninsula, and much more recently. When the Turks took possession of the country it was the glorious empire of the Czar Dushan that was sacrificed on the field of Kossovo to protect Europe. We alone threw off the oppressor without help. You blame us now for changing our dynasty in the old-fashioned way. What of your own regicidal acts, committed after centuries of freedom had given you time to grow peaceful, while our civilization was crushed five centuries ago, and kept at the point to which Europe had then arrived? We have never had a fair chance. Our nation is cut into four pieces, for Bosnia and Old Servia are ours, and Montenegro had never yielded to the Turk. Austria has hampered our trade, Russia has interfered with our politics, and we are not even allowed to have access to the sea."

Servia deserves sympathy. We must not blame the Serb if he talks too much of his past glory. When the Turkish extinguisher came down on the candle of Balkan civilization, it was Servia that had kindled the flame, and in the marble chapel of the ancient monastery of Studenitsa you may still see the embroidered banners and illuminated volumes of what was then one of the leading civilizations of the world. And of all the pitiable populations of European Turkey the Serbs of Old Servia are the greatest sufferers; that historic home of the race is rapidly becoming depopulated. Servia is denied, not only political unity but even economic liberty. She has no outlet to the sea, and Austria (being her only customer) can, and does, impose economic slavery. While Austria shuts her from the ocean and throws out a long arm to divide the two Servian branches of Servia and Montenegro, no wonder that annexation is planned in Macedonia. Servia must wait for the union of her race, but it is hard for her to wait.

The Bulgarian would not occupy the time allowed him, for he is a man of few words. At the most he would say: "The people of Macedonia call themselves Bulgarians, but we do not want their country. Only give them peace. They flood our labour markets, and their sufferings excite our people. Give them autonomy, or any decent government you like. We would rather, like the real mother before Solomon, give the whole child to some one else than see it divided."

He would say nothing of past glory or present culture. It is irksome to him to express pride or even gratitude, else he also might claim that twice in the last thousand years the Bulgarian Empire governed the peninsula; and more cogently he might speak of the astonishing progress of his country in the brief lifetime of one generation—of commerce, of agriculture, the political fame of Stambuloff, and the literary works of Vazof, translated into all the great languages of Europe.

The process of liberation has gone so far as to give each nation a footing upon free soil except one, Albania. This ancient people must not be lost to the comity of nations. Macedonia forms no homogeneous race specially distinguished from Greek or Serb, but Albania cannot be divided without destroying a nation. Albania has a history too: the Turk has kept her employed with tribal feud and vendetta, and divided her people in religious faith; but the Albanian is the least bigoted of zealots. I have even visited a chief who, though a Mohammedan, supported a Christian priest to serve an ancient chapel on his estate, and often joined in prayers for the protection of the patron saint. The Mohammedan convert among the Greeks and Slavs becomes a Turk, but an Albanian remains true to his nation's hopes. He is the ideally faithful retainer. If the traveller praises the Turk because he finds his Turkish servant so delightful, you will generally find that this Turk is an Albanian. He is often found among the ablest of Turkish Governors and the most devout of Roman Catholic priests. When relief was sent from England to keep alive those whom the Sultan intended to kill by starvation in 1903, it was the trusty Albanians who made the work possible.

With the Sick Man's estate waiting to be divided, what wonder if every possible claimant puts in an appearance? Even Roumania, though her frontiers do not touch Turkey, thinks it worth while to create something to bargain with at the final distribution, and she has a basis of claim in the Roumanian people of Macedonia, most of them wandering shepherds, but others prosperous tradesmen, who have created some of the wealthiest towns in the country.

The Greek, the Serb, the Bulgarian, the Roumanian, all endeavour to increase the number of their compatriots by means of churches and schools, financed largely by the respective Governments. The schoolmasters vie with each other in offering inducements to attend their school, so much so that the parent may sometimes not only get his children clothed and educated for nothing, but make an income also out of them, for instead of paying he receives a fee.

At times the spirit of chauvinism is thinly veiled under the garb of Churchmanship. No one can understand the outlook in Macedonia without realizing that nationalities are identified with Churches, combining to produce an intensity of nationalist feeling quite incredible to the Occidental. At periods like the years 1904–8 religion is degraded to the level of a pretext for exciting national zeal, and although the respective Churches make no pretence of differing to the smallest extent in theology or ritual, yet the hatred of heresy (which filled the West of Europe with war after the Reformation) is often used to fan the flame. The machinery of the Church is employed for the prosecution of rivalry. This strife must proceed in the barbarous atmosphere maintained by the Turk, and consequently also by the use of barbarous means. It would be as unfair to call these people unworthy, therefore, of liberty as it would be to say that Protestants and Catholics who fought in the seventeenth century were not capable of evolution or fit for the name of Christian.

Or, again, we are told that the races are too mixed for autonomy, so that the Turk had better stay. If these critics studied the statistics of Hungary or Austria or Switzerland, they would find those populations equally heterogeneous. Some disentanglement will be needed, but this is no more than the obvious task. The history of the last century is already the history of the disentanglement of races. Language is no difficulty, for all Macedonians are polyglot, and where whole families are accustomed to make an annual migration, movements of population are not impossible. Every liberation from Hungary to Crete has involved difficulties, and every liberation has brought disorder to an end.

Yet these last are not things which we condemn. When we incline to doubt if the Balkan peoples themselves do not make liberation futile, there is one unfailing index to show us whether "the pig makes the sty or the sty the pig." It is this: that in no single case has Turkish authority been removed without an immediate cessation of bloodshed and a growth of civilization which, in view of the past, is in some ways more amazing than that of Japan.

No Englishman blames rebellion against cruel tyranny, but we are sometimes told that if nations fail to get free it is because they have not fibre and pluck—they are not fit for freedom. For us who have nothing to suffer for a cause, and need not risk our lives, is this not a little mean? These people could all get protection and privilege if they denied their religion. As to pluck, their fault is rather that they are too daring. An Englishman who accompanied a band found himself eating his supper within two hundred yards of a Turkish picket. The rebels go to more than probable death. They carry poison lest they should be taken alive and be tortured. A band of fifteen was lately surrounded and found its retreat cut off. When cartridges were nearly exhausted, they hurriedly debated how to die. They asked the leader to shoot each in turn. He did so, and then blew out his own brains. A letter was found from one of the band to his mother, hoping she would forgive what trouble he had caused her when she heard how he gave his life.

Lady Thompson, travelling where she had previously distributed relief, asked after a certain deaf-mute boy. His mother for a few moments was unable to speak, then she said: "The Turks killed him. We did not find him at first. When the snow melted we found his cap. It was terrible! But we do not sorrow now—he died for his people."

There are nations to whom it is worth giving a chance to live—to make of themselves "nations that may create new types of character and new forms of literary and artistic life."

* * * * *

To dispose of the Macedonian problem two steps are needed—first, to find a scheme of government; secondly, to impose it upon the Turk. The former is clearly known, and it is not the inhabitants of Macedonia who make it unattainable. The second is the business of the Great Powers, and it is they who fail. The obstacle is their own jealousies and greeds.

Of the six Powers, one in particular might, in a reasonable world, be expected to protect her cousins the Southern Slavs. Russia was, in fact, in a fair way to deliver them, but England prevented her. If it had not been for the Crimean War and Mr. Disraeli's Berlin policy there would be no Macedonian problem now. In fear of Russia, we incited Austria to move southwards; by giving her Bosnia we directed her eyes towards Macedonia and the port of Salonica. But now that we have seen our mistake we halt between two policies, with the result that Russia and Austria took counsel together, and agreed in 1897 to divide European Turkey if the time should come.

Russia and Austria would at least put a stop to bloodshed, but they would encroach on the rights of other Powers, both great and small. Their present policy is merely one of delay. Each has her own difficulties at home, and would rather maintain the *status quo* till the Macedonian plum is ripe. Populations are more easily governed when they are exhausted. Events are paving the way, and it is enough if each Power can prevent the other from stealing a march.

These two Great Powers have shown some energy. They carry on a propaganda by liberal gifts to churches and monasteries, and by a display of sympathy now with one party among the Christians and now another. A favourite method of Russia is to encourage her agents to venturous courses, and repudiate them if they fail. Sometimes the Consul tries a domineering policy; hence the murder of a Russian Consul in 1903.

The novel feature of the situation is the intervention of Germany. The Kaiser's visit to Turkey and his famous address to his "good friend the Sultan" have created a belief that a definite policy of adventure in Turkey is being pursued. It is more likely that some keen spirits in the German Foreign Office, perhaps incited rather by hunters after profitable trade concessions than by patriotic Chauvinism, suggested the policy of fishing in troubled waters. Turkey is dying; why not get what you can before the death? Something could be made out of railways in Asia Minor, and the mines of Thasos are yielding a princely fortune. At all events, the policy would act as a sop to the trading classes in Germany, who have a grudge against the Emperor. So the Embassy at Constantinople became a banking-house. Colonies were founded in Asia Minor, the Bagdad Railway concession was obtained, and the Powers were cajoled into permitting an increase in the Turkish Customs duties, so as to finance the German scheme. Germany by obstructing reform posed as the Turk's friend, and got her reward. Her position as the protector of Turkey is similar to that which we held in 1878. Her aim has been less strategic and more commercial than ours.

Over against the three empires nursing the Sick Man, from whom they hope to inherit, stand the three Western Powers through whose democratic assemblies the humane instincts of the common people make themselves felt. Their interests, also, favour the welfare of the small Balkan nations, by whatever dispositions these may be promoted. But the Eastern Powers have the *status quo* on their side. France follows Russia. She drops her protectorate of the Eastern Christians, and gets big orders for the Creusot gun factory. Italy, whatever her adventures in Tripoli, must be at variance with her ally Austria. She fears an

Austrian port at the mouth of the Adriatic, and she cannot trust in Austria's promise to keep her hands off that country. She finances Albanian schools and builds a railway in Montenegro, the home of the Italian Queen, which will be useful to checkmate Austria's designs, though Austria's railways have had the start, and already bring her into measurable distance of a direct line to Salonica.

England, since she found (as Lord Salisbury put it) that she had "put her money on the wrong horse," has favoured the small Powers, and for Macedonia urges autonomy. But her voice is uncertain. Bulgaria, though we saved her from the vengeance of Russia in 1885, found that she could not rely upon us when Prince Alexander needed our support. English opinion is still confused by the historic question, "Shall Russia be allowed to possess the Dardanelles?" Government and people alike are swayed by the relics of party tradition. The Conservative faintly remembers that his party backed the Turk; the Liberal knows that Gladstone's contrary policy won the Liberal victory of 1880; but modern Toryism has attacked Young Turkey, and Liberalism tried to befriend her. It is no longer a party question. The most definite factor lies in the great but unsuspected numbers scattered over the country who are determined to atone for the result of our intervention in 1878. The Young Turks and their failure have destroyed the old pro-Turkism.

The nations of Europe are indifferent, but there is not so much active opposition as a certain *vis inertiæ*. What is lacking is a leader. The progress which Lord Lansdowne achieved in the face of a reluctant Europe is enough to show what a minister might do with circumstances improved as they already are. But the solution of the difficult knot does require a definite lead. It is not a question of offending other Powers, though in the past, for a fancied interest, we did not hesitate to resort even to arms. The threat of opposition from other Powers would bind us to inaction, yet what we have been deterred by hitherto is not the fear of war, but the desire to promote our other concerns. In 1904 we gave way to the French with the Moroccan agreement in view, and now we fear to spoil our relations with Russia. Material interests should be placed in proper relation to an obvious duty. Success depends on the preferences which we give to our proposals over other matters with which our relations to each Great Power are concerned.

CHAPTER III

THE CAUSE OF THE TROUBLE

The Turk an interloper—A reigning caste—His virtues—His patience—Why we like him—His faults—His government based on barbarous ideas—Inefficiency, corruption, inequality, cruelty

TURKISH government in the European provinces if lenient and just, might remain as a tolerated despotism. The failure of Young Turkey to provide tolerable conditions makes it fair that among the peoples with a claim to Macedonia we should omit the Turks. Have they no rights there from long possession, or from the fact that they are the present inhabitants? They have neither. So little have we been taught of Eastern history that we realize with difficulty what a newcomer the Turk is. The very houses we live in were, in thousands of cases, built before he entered Europe; not only houses accounted ancient: many even of our timber structures (and wood does not take long to decay) were already standing when

Constantinople fell. The Turk himself admits that he is but a stranger and an interloper in Europe. It is a saying with him that he has not come to settle, and to Asia he will return, but that as in blood he came so in blood will he go out. His prescriptive right to Salonica is no more than it was to Athens or Budapest.

And, again, the Turks are a mere governing caste. True, there are some Moslem villages in Macedonia, but even these are populated as a rule by Slavs converted to Islam, or are new settlements of Circassian colonists. Thus the feeling that the Turks have the natural right of a nation to express itself in government does not apply to Macedonia. If the principle of autonomy can anywhere be applied to the Turk, it would be in Anatolia, for there, in the west of Asia Minor, alone of all the lands of the empire, can a really Turkish population be found.

But even if Macedonia were largely Turkish there would still be need for liberation, for whether his subjects be Christian or Mohammedan, the Turk is unable to govern them. Here is the fundamental trouble. Mohammed's religion still has power to raise the savage tribes of Africa; but whereas Buddhism and Hinduism have done as much and given peace, Mohammedanism has in one respect at least been an affliction to the world, for it instilled a spirit of conquest, and the power to conquer, into nations unfit to govern.

It cannot be too often insisted that the question before us is one of government, and government alone. We are often told, in opposition to reform, that the Turk is a good-fellow. Very true; and if the question at issue were the social merit of peasants we have met on our travels, the real Turk would stand high. Only let us remember that we are concerned with politics, not with the social charm of individuals.

The Turk has many virtues. Among his own people he is quiet and kindly; truthful and devout, if intolerant; chaste according to Moslem chastity, and sober so long as he is ignorant. Those who, like Sir William Whittall, have searched his mind deeply, find there what they call a type of Irish humour, not, however, visible to the uninitiated. The Turk is lazy, but his love of repose in some shady garden, or in his summer-house over a murmuring stream, is a charming quality; his appreciation of *rahat*, or delight, if somewhat material, is certainly attractive.

And one marked virtue the Turk presents. In the Divine scheme of things the Turk was not meant for a ruler, but when the qualities of mankind come to be summed up in the final unity, one distinct contribution the Turk will have made. His part will be to present the beauty of patience. Not discipline, for when he is excited he loses his head completely. At the butchery at Kuklish in 1905 the Russian officer Captain Cimitiere begged the

Turkish officer to forbid his soldiers to kill girls. The officer replied that it would be useless to do so, for they did not know what they were doing. Neither is his quality one of loyalty, for many soldiers desert the army, and sometimes fly to infidel Bulgaria. Nor can he be called obedient, for the unique feature of Turkish administration is that the laws are not obeyed. But watch the tattered soldier standing in the snow to guard the railway line, by the side ot the wretched tent which has been his home for years, and you will see in the round, expressionless Osmanli face a quality which not even the stolidist European conscript could show for a week—a patience which, like the deplorable patience of women, appears sublime.

What is it in the Turk which appeals so strongly to the English? It is not his simple and rural character, for then we should logically find our ideal in people such as the Boers; the Turk is, like them, distinguished by his hatred of "progress," and his narrow, puritanical faith. Rather it is the pride of a conquering race and the favourable light in which the dominant man appears among a group of apparently weaker people. And the Turk, too, has a tradition of hospitality. The Beys love to overfeed their guests, though in this respect they are behind the Albanians. Not that the Christian is any less hospitable when he has the chance, but in Turkey he seldom has. And in a country where travelling means a succession of physical discomforts, you naturally remember with most pleasure the man who could relieve your fatigue and hunger.

With the English, too, there is a tradition of friendship towards old comrades in arms. And to all lovers of the picturesque there is a charm in a people, and even in a government, which preserves outwardly the features of the Middle Age. Curiously enough, however, this confidence is misplaced. In this case efficiency is not the alternative to beauty. The advent of progressive government (whether the Turk has given way to the Greek or the Slav) does not, as elsewhere, mean the destruction of the picturesque. The wealthy Turk of the town does, indeed, build his house with an eye to beauty. The plaster brackets of his deeply projecting windows delightfully follow Mr. Watts's example in using simulation to heighten architectural effects; but outside the towns the squalor and poverty of the dwellings puts them far below the level of the picturesque, whereas in free countries the houses are built, not only with a more solid air of comfort, but with deeper eaves and shadier verandas.

As a peasant the Turk is attractive, as peasants almost always are. It is in government that he becomes intolerable. Before the advent of the telegraph the old school of Governors, though ignorant, had often initiative and a certain honesty. The telegraph and the industrious suspicion of Abdul Hamid introduced in their place a class of office-bred functionaries, with no local responsibility, because to avoid the chance of trouble from rebellious Governors like Ali Pasha, they were so frequently moved. The new school speak French, wear frock-coats, and have often displayed a certain knowledge of the West.

But to speak of the balance of criminality when debating the merits of Moslem and Christian governments is to throw doubt on all the chief beliefs which have raised the human race—the belief, namely, that all races and religions are equally entitled to justice, order, freedom, to the protection of life and property and family honour; that intellect, art, and material wealth should be developed; that a man should have one wife only; that women have souls equally with men; that children should be revered; that uncorrupt government is good and violence bad.

Educated Turks would adopt these standards, but the old-fashioned Moslem denies such rights and principles. What he might have been if Mohammedanism had not closed his mind before he came in contact with Christianity we may see to-day from the Hungarians, people of the same blood but among the most progressive of the earth.

Again, the Turk is not even a good Asiatic. What culture he has was borrowed from other races, and now he has lost both borrowed art and native vigour. The splendid ruins of mosque or caravanserai, disappearing among the squalid cottages of to-day, prove in how incredibly short a time the morale of the first Turkish conquerors has disappeared. Without foreign aid the empire would have long ago collapsed.

There is a class of enthusiasts who contend that while the Indian government remains autocratic, we have no right to complain of Turkey. But does not the security of life and honour come before the attainment of nationalist ideals? Some hold, again, that the state of Russia is worse than that of Turkey. But the Russian bureaucracy in normal times supplies order and the possibility of a decent life; no comparison can be made between the Armenians in Turkey and the prosperous and cultured Armenians in Russia. Even if this were not so, the comparison would be idle, for the two governments are based on wholly different conceptions, and have wholly different potentialities. It would be as absurd to say that the government of the Tudors, because it was brutal, was not capable of improvement, as to say that any European government is as hopeless as that of the Turk.

Turkish government is, first, inefficient. Some of the richest lands of Europe, once the granary of Rome, lie idle for want of the simplest elements of common-sense administration—of roads, of safety, of regular taxation. "Where the Turkish hoof treads the grass never grows." The Turk cannot see even the most obvious course in which his own interests lie. His stupidity may be observed even in our own country. When some particularly monstrous massacre has been reported, he continues to send to such English newspapers as will publish it the bare statement that the whole report is an undiluted fabrication, incorrigibly blind to the way in which English people regard him.

Needless to say, his government is largely incapable from laziness; but considering what it is, that is perhaps a virtue. From the first the Turk was compelled to employ the intelligence of his Christian subjects, and therefore to be tolerant to their Churches. He is spasmodic.

In spite of the efforts of many Young Turks the government is still corrupt. The stories of which the Turks are so fond make frequent fun of the invariable corruption of prefects and judges. The trader lets himself be robbed and gives up business rather than pay to the judges more than he would gain by a favourable verdict.

The peasant regards corruption as the chief characteristic of his government. One of the most charming peasants I have ever met was a Turkish yeoman in Bosnia. He praised the Austrian rule, and I asked him, as a good Mohammedan, whether he did not prefer the Sultan's government. He replied in broken German (which he had learned from the Austrian soldiers): "I love the Sultan, but in his country the great men are always thieves."

There might be hope of reform if the Moslem were not invincibly attached to his ascendancy, to the fundamental principle that as against the Mohammedan the Christians have not equal rights. To him they are *rayah*—*i.e.*, cattle. This claim vitiates all the promises of equality with which Europe has allowed itself to be put off. There is no cause for wonder in this, but only in the fact that, after so long experience, there were Europeans who thought it worth while to extract the promises. The laws of Turkey are on European lines, but in practice the Turk is above the law. Murder, rape, kidnapping, land-grabbing go unpunished day after day.

A Blue Book touches the spot where this unequal treatment most profoundly exasperates the Christian mind. Vice-consul Captain Townsend reports that the people grow accustomed to having their bread, &c., taken by the soldiers, "but they can never reconcile themselves to outrages on their women."

A corrupt, incapable, and unjust government may be tolerated if it is mild; but Turkish rule is cruel as well. In times of disturbance troops must not be judged too closely, but we can hardly overlook the killing of women and children. I myself have seen a child disfigured with wounds inflicted with a sword—that is to say, by an officer—and a woman blinded by knife-wounds two years after the Young Turkish era. An English officer during the insurrection of 1903 found a woman still alive who had been partly flayed—an incident not typical of peace and rarely, one may hope, of war.

It is more important to judge a Government by its conduct in ordinary times. If your views are not known and you can speak Turkish, a little conversation with the soldiers of your escort will soon dissipate any doubt you may feel as to the truth of sensational rumours. To rape, to kill, and to burn houses appears to them the only sensible way to deal with a people whose unrest has dragged the Turkish soldier from his Asiatic home.

NOTE.—For details, see Appendix.

CHAPTER IV

REFORM BY SUASION

The Concert rejected control and adopted supervision—The sole alteration—Disorder not diminished—The British district—Officers powerless—Troops promote disorder—Examples of outrage—A sacked village—European opinion

UNTIL 1903 the threats of revolution in Macedonia were not taken seriously. Diplomacy refused to believe that the rebels could give trouble, and the annual warning of a rising in the spring became a subject for mockery. But in 1903 the rebels drove the Governments of Europe to an effort they had hoped to avoid. The European coach began to move. Some of the horses jibbed, but one was for going full speed; the result was a moderate pace. Two courses presented themselves to the diplomats: the first was to save themselves trouble and maintain their dignity, to snub the busybodies, to keep things outwardly peaceful for a few years more; the second was to grasp the nettle, not to be afraid to admit that the rebellious Macedonians had forced their hands—in fact, to go full pace and get the journey over. This course commended itself to that class of minds which desires not only to maintain the peace of Europe and induce the revolutionary bands to go home, but actually to remove the source of disturbance and to secure the possibility of a decent life for the Macedonian peasant. To this latter class, happily, belonged Lord Lansdowne; but prejudice demanded that the Government should go slowly. So the piecemeal policy was adopted; control of Macedonian affairs was not insisted on, and in its place we were given the policy of supervision. European officers were sent to watch the proceedings of the gendarmerie, and later on a Commission representing the Powers was established to examine the finances.

It is impossible for anyone who saw for himself the state of things in Macedonia, and made friends among the agents of the Powers concerned, not to conclude that Lord Lansdowne was right in his proposal for real control by the European Powers. There was neither reform nor sufficient pretence of it to avoid the danger of war. Yet the Turks profited by the situation to wring from the Powers a great financial concession. They obtained an increase in the amount of the tariff varying from 37 to 11 per cent, while the Powers gained nothing except the confirmation of a scheme of reform already proved ridiculous, and the satisfaction of bolstering up their own pride.

But let us give every possible credit to the scheme. There was one tangible fact that apologists for the scheme could point to—viz., that the Turkish officials and troops did actually receive their pay. This should doubtless result in better conduct to the subject people; they are not compelled to steal, and they are more likely to accept some discipline from their officers.

The gendarmerie schools for non-commissioned officers established at the capital of each province, had lecturers for teaching medicine, law, and religion. They hoped (to use their own charming phrase) to make what was once a curse to the country the sign and symbol of paternal government.

Again, the Financial Commission achieved the dismissal of some minor officials, and had in hand some money for building roads, at the time conspicuously absent.

Even among those who have not with their own eyes seen burned houses and bayoneted children the failure of the reforms was not concealed. He is driven to claim that brigands in want of work no longer donned gendarmerie uniform and passed as regular members of the force. I remember the chastened utterance of a Turkish official attached to the Finance Commission, who told me how the tone of Turkish functionaries had been improved by the

Commission's influence. "We Turks," he said, "are beginning to see that we have learnt many good things from Europe without losing our dignity; chemistry and astronomy, for instance: why should we not now learn government also?" One of our Consuls did certainly claim that great improvement had taken place in the conduct of the Turkish beys; but when I asked to what particular feature of the reforms this might be due, he confessed that he thought the most probable influence was fear of the rebel bands! A European who farms in Macedonia thought things slightly improved. "How?" I said. "Well, the Turkish murder committees have got the peasants well in hand."

If success could anywhere be shown, it was in the district of Drama, allotted to the British officers, and always quoted as proof of success. So far, however, from proving the argument, it is Drama that furnishes the final evidence of failure, for here everything favoured reform. There were no rebel bands, but a peaceful population. As you ride from Drama to Kavalla, things appear on the very surface increasingly un-Turkish, almost laughably European. You are actually on a tolerable road. Landaus full of tobacco merchants constantly pass. No one carries a rifle. Strangest of all, a fast-trotting mail-cart plies daily; and when you have crossed the low hills where St. Paul passed on his way to Philippi, you are suddenly in the Italian Riviera.

Kavalla lies below you for all the world like Monte Carlo, with its ancient walls encircling the rocky town, with its villas and tennis-courts, with the yacht of an Austrian Grand Duke, and big European factories.

The Turk is specially anxious to humour the English, whom he regards as the most dangerous leaders of the reform movement. He was ready to make concessions because the area concerned is small and no great problems are involved. And, greatest of all favourable conditions, you had the English officer—the best qualified of all human creatures to impress the Turk; the man the Turk still somehow trusts to protect him from the Russian and the Bulgarian; the man he admires for his open-handed generosity and power to dominate; the man who makes even Moslems like him and obey him; the strong, genial man to whom in his heart he cringes.

And yet even in Drama you had countless murders and disorders; you had the gendarmerie themselves used for hunting recruits, instead of preventing crime, and attempts made to deter the officers from even visiting, much less reforming, the prisons.

But it is the rest of Macedonia which matters more, and there disorder was infinitely worse. The general fact which vitiated the whole scheme of the Powers is that the armed force of the country was beyond the control of the foreign officers, and that even if the work of the soldier and the gendarme were perfect, the courts of justice are without even inspection The plan of the Powers, while supervising the gendarme (or rather a part of it), left prefect and judge to arrest whom they like, to keep in prison or to torture him, without even inquiry, much less interference, on the part of Europeans.

Not only was the gendarmerie inadequate to cope with misrule, not only were Europeans debarred from all investigation into the conduct of the police in towns, but the rural gendarmes, to whom the supervision is limited, were specifically misused. They were largely employed in tax-collecting—that is, they were lent to those who have bought the tithe for more than it ought legally to produce, in order to help them rob the peasants. There were not enough left for patrolling the roads. They were engaged in collecting reservists, and at one lonely inn at which I dismounted there were twelve such prisoners, guarded by seven gendarmes.

Equally intolerable is the normal encroachment by the army upon the proper duties of the gendarmerie. Soldiers are not supposed to do duty among the peasants except as assistants to the gendarmerie, but in point of fact they are used to overawe the people. They are stationed in innumerable villages, nominally to control the rebel bands. How far they are likely to succeed may be judged from the fact that most of them, being Turks from Asia Minor, are unable to understand the languages of Macedonia. Hilmi Pasha was lately asked how it was that the troops so seldom caught the rebels. "The bands," he replied, "work by night, the troops by day; hence it is that they seldom meet." The business they are really sent to perform they do most efficiently: they go from house to house demanding hidden rifles, and if neither money nor rifles are forthcoming, they beat and bully the people.

Europe was put off in February, 1903, by the talk of Christians being enrolled in the gendarmerie. An instance may suffice to show the value of this reform. Occasionally, though rarely, a Christian gendarme was allowed a rifle. As a protest against this, one of these privileged Christians was lately attacked by a Turkish peasant in the street. To give the alarm and save his life the gendarme fired his rifle into the air. To set an example to Christians in general, he was sent to prison for three months.

But the proof of the pudding is in the eating. Defects of organization matter less than the peasant's life and his daughter's honour. To test the success of the Powers and their scheme, we have only to ask whether outrages ceased. In Turkey there are no statistics worth reading, and the only evidence we can trust is to be found in the reports of Consuls and gendarmerie officers, or in the evidence of our own eyes. The chances are so remote that a traveller among the 5,000 villages of Macedonia will come upon the worst outrages, that incidents within his own experience are the strongest proof that worse things prevail. I discard the details of bloodshed and rape with which every European resident is familiar, and limit myself to facts strictly verified.

Even in the district of the French officers, which was comparatively peaceful, some forty murders were reported to their energetic head, Colonel Verrand, every month. At Uskub a murder occurred in the open market of the city, which attracted considerable comment—not because murder is rare, but by its picturesque simplicity. A Bulgarian merchant had ordered a pair of boots from a Turkish bootmaker; when the boots arrived they did not fit, so the Bulgarian called upon the bootmaker, who was sitting at the open front of his shop in the bazaar, and complained that the boots must be altered. The Turk replied by picking up his heavy chopper and cleaving the skull of his customer. By way of showing administrative activity, two other Bulgarians were arrested for the murder, but the Turk carries on his business in prosperity.

Among the incidents reported by the Italian General De Georgis was a more melancholy story. Twelve young girls, leaving school together, were set upon and the whole party killed.

A government must be judged by its power to keep unruly subjects in order. What, then, shall we say to an administration which commits crimes itself? If every murderer were efficiently caught by the gendarmerie, there would still be little public order if he were at once let free by the authorities and innocent people thrown into prison. One of the greatest absurdities of the so-called reforms was that the European officers had no control of the gaols. At Uskub a new prison had been built, but the untried prisoners, many of them arrested months before their case comes on for trial, were kept underground in even worse quarters than the convicted criminals. Here the innocent and the guilty were crammed together. In some of the prisons there was not even room to lie down at night, and the dead were taken out daily. Yet so great are the difficulties put in the way of the foreign officers that no regular visitation of the prisons by them takes place at all.

The presence of Europeans, however, has had some effect; they may congratulate themselves on having compelled the Turks to develop a new administrative art—namely, the manufacture of false evidence. The French officers had occasion to notice a particularly fine example of this species of Turkish humour. Some young Christians, of more means than their neighbours, in a specially peaceful district near the coast of Macedonia, unwarily asked permission to go out quail-shooting. While enjoying themselves on the plain, some common soldiers came upon them, took their guns from them, and gave them a sound thrashing, though they produced the permit of the Governor to go out shooting. To the subtle humour of the Governor's mind this appeared an opportunity not to be lost, either to break the pride of the Christians or to extort baksheesh for himself; but as the prisoners held his own permit, some other pretext must be found for charging them with a crime. Fortunately for the Governor, at the same time a corpse was found in the woods. It mattered little that the spot was in a remote ravine many miles from the plain where the men had been shooting quails, or that the cause of death was a large bullet obviously not fired from a shot-gun. These incongruities only added to the fun of flouting the European supervisors, and the unfortunate sportsmen remained in prison.

So early as 1904 we had begun to hope that serious outrages by the troops had become rare. Parliament was informed that the slaughter in February, 1905, at the village of Kuklish, was quite an exception. The Financial Commission, since established, had, one hoped, at all events put an end to such major enormities. Nine months after the Financial Commission had been established a large party of Turkish regular troops, not without authority from its officers, marched out for a deliberate looting expedition against a village near Vodena named Rodevo. Nearing the village in the early dawn, they caught three peasants in the fields, tied their hands together, and ordered them to lead the way to the village. In the dusk the inhabitants thought that a band of brigands was attacking the village, and rushed out of their houses. The soldiers fired upon them, and did not leave the village until ten people had been killed and a number of houses burnt to the ground.

Murders and massacres are not committed in the presence of tourists with the escort of cavalry which is inflicted upon them. Even the intelligence of a Turk is equal to the task of postponing outrages till the foreigner has passed. But it was evident, even as one rode through the country, that disorder, far from being suppressed, had even increased since the "reforms." Five years before it was not usual to carry a rifle in Macedonia; now every Turkish landlord rode with his Martini across his saddle. At the once wealthy town of Krushevo, where the houses destroyed three years ago are still for the most part melancholy ruins, we were taken to see a wounded man. He was a man of means, with a fine house. He had been working in his beautiful garden, which overhangs a little stream, when a bullet from a window opposite laid him low. The bullet mark upon the stone showed where he had been standing, close to his fig-tree. An act, you say, of ordinary private feud;

but these things happen day after day and the murderer goes free.

* * * * *

When we arrived at Monastir the Inspector-General had issued orders that no travellers were to be allowed outside the town. It was not convenient that Europe should hear any more of villagers still starving among the ruins of their homes. In case the tourist should claim the privilege of free travel demanded by his passport, and venture to ride through the country without an escort, stringent orders had been issued that any man who supplied us with horses would do so at his peril. It was not impossible, however, to find horses over whose owner the Turks had no control, and we rode out to see for ourselves a village which had been sacked three days before, an incident typical of the present state of things. Finding we had started, the authorities sent an escort after us, for if any foreigner is taken by brigands the Turk has to pay.

The large village of Smilevo lies at the head of a long steep valley, where three beautifully wooded combes come down from the higher mountains to form a little river. Most of the houses had been burnt by the Turks as punishment for the insurrection of 1903, but a great number had been well rebuilt, for the men of Smilevo are noted builders. They are employed in many parts of Macedonia, returning for the winter to Smilevo, which before the insurrection was a prosperous village of 2,000 souls.

On Sunday, September 9, at five o'clock we were watching a magnificent sunset from the hill above Prilep, a few miles from Smilevo. Little did we imagine what devilries were proceeding so near. At that moment the village found itself surrounded by armed men. The band consisted of Turks and of Greeks, who, coming from Greece, had no knowledge of the district, but who were ready enough to take advantage of Turkish protection and wipe out old scores against the Bulgarians. A number of the villagers who were in the inn hurriedly consulted what to do. On the chance of obtaining mercy they sent a deputation to the leader of the band on the slope above the village, carrying water-melons for him and his men. The chief replied to their prayers: "I do not want water-melons; I want blood." There was no time for the villagers to organize resistance. The bandsmen were already plundering houses and shooting at random those they found in them. It was a wild and horrible medley that passed that beautiful Sunday evening, for the band included Turks from neighbouring villages, whose aim was to loot, while the object of the leaders was to terrorize and kill. Among the wounded, whom we afterwards saw, was a young married woman dreadfully hacked about the head; her fingers also were lacerated. When she saw the band she ran to call the cattle.

The bandits, seeing that she was wearing the coins and rings that form the dowry of the richer peasants, began to tear the rings from her fingers. As a last hope she offered them money, and having, fortunately, £3 in her pocket, she saved her life. Another woman escaped by a ruse. Her husband was away, and hoping to frighten the bandsmen, whom she saw from the window, she turned towards an inner room and called out, "Bring the gun," upon which the ruffians passed on to find easier prey. In some houses men, women, and children too, must have resisted frantically. There were at least thirty bullet marks on the wall of one room and others on the floor, and there was blood upon a heavy wooden block where some one had been killed with an axe used for chopping firewood. Ten houses were set on fire, and the band did not leave until nine men and women were dead, and four small children.

Two days after, the Russian and Austrian Consuls visited the place, and found a child of nine with five wounds still alive. Six other wounded were carried on ponies some eight hours' journey to Monastir, where, for want of a hospital, they were laid in the little houses of Bulgarian artisans.

As we walked through the village a fine young man with a peculiarly English type of face pointed to the still smouldering remains of what had been a large stone house, and said: "Here was my shop and my home; what am I to do now?" We were accompanied by a number of villagers and by the Turkish Prefect of the neighbouring town, who had come over to collect information. He complained that the villagers were leaving the place in unnecessary fear. He had tried in vain to persuade them that the Government promised complete protection, and he was much aggrieved that they would not listen. Some twenty soldiers were also in the place. They belonged to the garrison situated on the hills above, where, as usual, the troops had sat fast until the killing was finished. We asked the Prefect if there was a church. He replied that there was, though it had been slightly damaged in the insurrection. We insisted on seeing it, and found the remains of a very large stone church, completely gutted from end to end. The dead were already buried in the churchyard. The latest grave made that day appeared so curiously small that we asked how old the child had been. We learnt that it was the body of a man, but burnt to a small cinder. Numbers of villagers had already left the village, and others were leaving. As we rode along we met a party consisting of an elderly woman and her four daughters. In front of them a man led two donkeys, almost invisible under an immense load of household utensils. On one side was a sack containing a large pig, on the other were mattresses and cooking-pans, while the women carried sieves and weaving utensils and bundles of live chickens tied together by the legs. We asked why these people were leaving the village by the circuitous route through the mountains, and found the reason to be that the only road down the valley from Smilevo lay through the Turkish village, from which had come the murderers themselves. We rested ourselves and our horses in this very village, hospitably entertained with water-melon and junket by one of the prosperous Turks of the place. The only ornaments on the walls of his room were a Martini rifle and a cartridge-belt; most of the cartridge-holders in the belt were empty.

We saw the surviving wounded at Monastir. The least severely injured was a handsome young man, who lay in a little veranda while his mother and his fiancée, who had also been wounded, fanned the flies away from his face. His hand had been shot through and mortification was beginning. A Bulgarian doctor who, after endless delay, had obtained permission to practise at Monastir, was trying to persuade the mother to allow of amputation, but she could not bear to think of her good-looking son without an arm. Next morning, when the gangrene had spread to the elbow, she yielded; but the operation could not take place without the appliances in the Turkish hospital, and the hospital director would not admit the boy without an order from the Governor. It was already more than doubtful whether mortification had not gone too far. Twenty-four hours were lost in obtaining the order. Within a few days all our wounded friends, except three, were dead.

* * * * *

The greatest evil of the situation was, perhaps, that the mind of Europe should know what was going on and be content to think that these things may be left to continue. The least was probably the ignominious position to which the able representatives of the Powers are obliged to submit, yet this is a matter of no small importance. When the scheme of reforms was accepted by the Turks they expected that the Powers meant business; but Hilmi Pasha is a clever man, and as soon as the Powers showed themselves willing to accept a small rebuff he was quick to follow up the advantage. He soon had the Financial Commission well in hand, as the following story, entirely believed among European residents, will adequately indicate: When the Pasha moved his Court from Salonica to Monastir for the summer season, he invited the Financial Commission to join him in his special train. But before they reached the station the astute Oriental had started on his journey. The Commissioners therefore did not put in an appearance when their chairman made his formal entry into Monastir. Important business was put through before they could arrive, and a staggering blow had been dealt at their prestige.

* * * * *

European diplomacy set out two years ago, primarily, no doubt, to prevent war, but professedly to establish order. Did it succeed? The opinion of Europeans on the spot was emphatic on this point. One expected to find them admitting that improvement was not complete. One was not prepared for the assertion, which was everywhere made, that, though the Turkish official and soldier have profited, because they are paid, the peasants, for whom reform was intended, are actually worse off than before. And this astonishing statement they support by the fact that taxation is far higher and the frequency of outrage is distinctly greater. If one class of danger to the peasant was diminished, another class was increased. It was always doubtful for the Macedonian Christian, when he went to his work in the fields, whether he would come back to find his property gone or his wife's honour lost; but now it was doubtful whether he and they would not have their throats cut while they were gathering in the crops. And yet, with all this horrid sacrifice, not even the selfish aim of Europe was obtained, for a Turco-Bulgarian war, with all the danger which it involves for the Great Powers, was more likely than ever.

To diplomats in comfortable quarters the "right of supervision" seemed something that should satisfy the demands of Parliaments and peoples. If they had seen with their own eyes what was happening in the villages, they would not have thought extravagant the conclusion expressed by one of the leading European officers: "C'est une comédie dégoûtante."

CHAPTER V

REFORM BY COERCION

European control essential—Different forms of it—Annexation—Autonomy—Control by the Concert—Each would bring peace—The practical problem—A definite proposal

FOR four years following the revolution Turkey was left an entirely free hand. At the end of that period her subjects in Europe were more dissatisfied than ever, and the various races had been driven to sink their differences in mutual defence. There was talk of European officials, and even of renewed intervention by the Concert, as the only alternative to chaos and war. It is therefore important to remind ourselves of former days and to judge from the recorded results of "reforms" under European supervision.

It is a strange illustration of the ways of diplomacy that not only after the Crimean War and the great crisis of 1878, but also in 1903 and 1905, the promise of self-reform was put forward to allay European public feeling. It is the offer of a stone in place of bread, and were it not justified by the ignorance of the public, it would be insulting to their intelligence.

In 1856 the Sublime Porte was crafty enough to issue a formal declaration embodying the promise of so-called rights to the Christian populations. This was known as the Hatti Humayum. As a matter of course, it remained a dead-letter, because, as every diplomat knows, the Mohammedan cannot contravene the central idea on which his position is based—viz., his ascendancy over the unbeliever. If the Sultan were to break this sacred law he would not be obeyed; he would be assassinated by his own people if he threw away their essential privilege, unless compelled to do by stronger Powers. In that case the "Sunna" commands him to yield, "lest damage ensue to Islam." At different periods, seeing that the game was up, he has desired such coercion in order to make concession possible, and has even asked for it. But without coercion and European control reform is in the nature of things impossible.

For the same reason the scheme of reform which Lord Salisbury achieved in 1896 has also proved a farce. It provided for Christian Assistant-Governors, who should act as a check upon the Turkish Governors with whom they sat. No one not wholly ignorant of the facts believed for a moment that these men, being Turkish subjects, would exercise a vestige of influence against Turkish claims, and they soon acquired the name of "Evetji"—that is to say, "Yes-Men," because their judgment has never been known to differ from that of their chiefs.

Thus Mr. Gladstone spoke only the words of common-sense when he said, speaking of the Turkish governing classes : " Bag and baggage, the Turk must go." What, then, is the right alternative to his rule? The answer is simple. Any plan is right which removes the supreme Turkish authority. Every system which has embodied this condition has proved successful, from aristocracy in Egypt and Bosnia to the excessive democracy of Greece. The only practical question is as to what plan is most easily achieved. Shall it be occupation by the great empires, control by the Concert, self-government, or partition among the small States.

The first has brought peace to Bosnia and Egypt, and parts of Turkey which are not fit for self-rule will eventually share the fate of those provinces. Such are Mesopotamia, Tripoli, Kurdestan, and perhaps Palestine.

Control by the Concert embodies the ideal for such international cities as Constantinople, and possibly Salonica—conceivably, also, for Armenia ; but when applied to territories like Crete and Eastern Roumelia, the Powers have found it difficult to co-operate, and unless the country occupied can ultimately govern itself they are loath to run the risk of a failure.

Happily, self-government is feasible in all European Turkey. Its populations have proved themselves fit to rule, and an autonomy which has succeeded so well in Hungary, Roumania, Servia, Greece, Montenegro, and Bulgaria would provide no less a feasible solution for Albania and Macedonia.

Annexation by a neighbouring small State was the fortunate fate of Thessaly, and is the obvious destiny for Old Servia and Epirus.

Reviewing these four methods in turn, the province under discussion here, so far from offering an insoluble problem, might be dealt with by any one of them; but its people would bitterly resent the first—namely, absorption in a great empire.

The plan professedly adopted in principle by the Great Powers was that of control by the Concert, and for this reason it found widespread support among the friends of freedom throughout Europe. It avoids the difficult question of the ultimate fate of Macedonia, reserving the choice between autonomy and partition to a later day. It aims at removing, as in the Lebanon, the direct rule of the Sultan by establishing a Government responsible to the Powers. The Powers advanced some distance along this road. Their military officers are established all over the country, and their Commissioners of Finance in the capital; the machinery of control was ready, and needed only the fuel of executive power to make it effective. In this direction lay the only hope of avoiding war. Macedonia, if not a racial unity, is a geographical entity, with one of the greatest of natural seaports for its centre. The alternative—Bulgarian conquest—would be much more distasteful to each minority than the impartial rule of the Powers. Resistance to reform on the part of the Turks is suicidal. The Turkish landlords in Macedonia know this, and would welcome a just control for they suffer from disorder. It is the officials who obstruct the way, because they would lose the profits of corruption.

It must not be forgotten that control was within an ace of being established. In 1903 Lord Lansdowne proposed it in the form of a Christian Governor. In 1905 he suggested a Commission representing the Powers, and had it not been for the Russo-Japanese war, and the unwillingness of France to go beyond the wishes of her Russian ally, it would then have been achieved, on the proposal of England, France, and Italy. The form which a practicable control would take is best expressed in Lord Lansdowne's own words: "The Commission would be given administrative and executive powers, and would, in the first instance, be instructed to frame without delay schemes for the effective contro of the administration of finance and justice." The kernel lies in the word "executive." Sir Edward Grey advanced the same principle in 1908.

In the Lebanon the very same judicial institutions that fail so completely under the Sultan work with perfect smoothness under a Governor controlled by the Powers.

European control would bring peace. Once the Sultan had accepted the reglement giving power to the Commissioners, recalcitrant Governors and corrupt judges would be dismissed. The troops would be confined to certain places. The police would be organized, as in Crete, by officers of the Powers.

Crime would then for the first time be punished and the innocent acquitted. With the roads improved and security provided, every market in the country would begin to grow. The Turkish Bey, reluctant to put away his rifle and give up the right of shooting his neighbour, would accept the inevitable when he found that along with these humiliations he was able to visit his remotest farms and to impose larger rents. The Christian peasant would find that he could till the fields in peace, and bring up his family in honour.

There are those who argue that government will be made impossible by the rebel bands, but the rebels will find their employment gone. The villagers are ready enough to support them now, because they offer some protection from the Turks, and help to relieve them from intolerable insults; but when these things are changed the villager will not give them his last loaf, as he often does now, for they will no longer be doing anything to improve his situation. Moreover, the revolutionary committee referred to—*i.e.*, the Bulgarian—is a democratic organization, controlled by the peasants, who elect its leaders. The ordinary outlets for the vigour of an active man in commerce and the professions, till now artificially closed, will prove a sufficient attraction to men who have often been driven to brigandage for want of any equally profitable trade. It is safe to prophesy that, before the Powers have provided order for a month, the most ruffianly of the rebel bands will have been dispersed.

Control would not commit the Powers to permanent responsibility. The country is adapted to partition, but its population is at the same time potentially homogeneous. Autonomy upon the Swiss system of cantons would meet its ethnological needs, and the cause of "Macedonia for the Macedonians" would doubtless become more and more popular.

There are two questions for the disinterested Governments of Europe. They are not, What Government would pacify the Macedonians? but How can the Turks be compelled to accept it? and How shall we persuade other Powers to act with us in demanding authority for the Commission already established, so that we may not have the odium of acting alone? Complete unity of action is not required for coercion. In the historic precedent of 1880, when Mr. Gladstone proposed to enforce the cession of Thessaly, two Powers alone were willing to join with us; it was only essential that the other Powers should not actively obstruct us. The situation is in one respect more favourable to-day, for the question is already on the European table; in 1880 there was no crisis to bring it forward. Coercion in favour of concerted control is not a wild-cat proposal. It has been formally made both by Lord Lansdowne and Sir Edward Grey.

A source of alarm, however, has been found in the fact of Pan-Islamic feeling in Egypt and India, and it is, no doubt, important to inquire whether this is better met by concession or by firm resistance. If the latter course is preferred by Sir Edward Grey, as would appear from his treatment of the Tabah question, then the same principle will equally apply to other quarrels with Turkey. It is interesting that the great Ambassador Sir William White wrote, so long ago as 1885, "We cannot shape our course in Europe by purely Asiatic considerations." The Moslems are hardly anywhere a majority in India, and they are profoundly divided, for the Shiahs, probably half of the Indian Mohammedans, entirely reject the Sultan's claim to the khalifate. Lord Salisbury did not hesitate to offend the supporters of Abdul Hamid. It is not defeat but victory that rouses Islamic feeling. The Indian Mutiny followed our actual armed alliance with Turkey and the Indian Moslems joined in it. Asiatic unrest is the result of an Asiatic victory—that of Japan.

What means of pressure upon other Governments a Foreign Minister may possess the public can never tell, for foreign affairs are kept surrounded with mystery, but that particular levers and obligations can be used as a means of persuasion is obvious. The diplomatic records of coercion from 1880 to 1905 are sufficient to show this; nor are other conditions absent which must be met before the Foreign Office can take action. There must be first the indication of support from public opinion and from the House of Commons. The former has never been wanting since 1902, and, whereas Lord Lansdowne was willing to act without the sympathy of either the Cabinet or the House, Sir Edward Grey is supplied with both. Lord Lansdowne, with all his disadvantages, practically forced the hands of the unwilling empires; and it is clear that throughout the vast field of interests and counter-interests which constitute the foreign relations of Great Britain there is no lack of material for arriving at agreement with inactive Powers.

Of some such materials it is desirable that the public should form an opinion. A suggestion made by Professor Westlake and other great international lawyers is that Great Britain should intimate to the Powers that, in the event of any proposal for European control in Macedonia being declined, she will refuse to join in any further effort of the reactionary Powers to prevent or limit war between the Balkan States and Turkey.

Professor Westlake further insisted that, should the Powers be unwilling to join us, and should war break out, the urgency of the problem and our special responsibility impose on us the duty of assisting the Balkan States with the resources which our overwhelming sea power gives us.

If it be answered that the fear of war breaking out may still prove inadequate to move the Concert, we must remember that Macedonia does not, like Armenia, depend on the Concert for its liberation. There are the armies of the small States at hand prepared, not only to occupy the country but to take over its government, and able to deal with the Turkish army if it is not reinforced from Asia. The Turks are extremely vulnerable by sea. The expulsion of the Turks is thus within reach of any naval Power which is ready to support the small States. Even the weakest naval Power could occupy custom-houses, under cover of naval guns, and prevent troopships from proceeding to Macedonia or to Arabia, thus paralysing Turkey without the need of landing armies. Those of the small States would act by land.

This policy would be fittingly accompanied by a self-denying ordinance, such as was made by England and France on the eve of the Crimean War, a public declaration that on no account would they turn the war to their private advantage.

Imagine, however, the worst to happen and war to break out. Is that worse than the present situation? The salient facts to-day are these: Firstly, that the disorder now prevailing is in effect a war, and of a kind even more terrible than formal hostilities, for it involves, not so much the contest of armed men as the killing of defenceless women and children. Secondly, war is inevitable in any case, since diplomacy despairs of establishing control without it. This being so, it is quite inconceivable that Macedonia, while the powerful army of her kinsmen in Bulgaria is encouraged by military observers to believe that it can beat the Turks, will be permanently left unavenged. The Powers, in effect, expect a war, and though they have not the vigour to prevent it, they dread the danger of its spreading into Europe. The tradition of diplomacy deprecates any but negative movements, yet it was inaction, not action, that caused the Russo-Turkish War, and the Power which shall undertake the leadership in the inevitable change will have secured Europe, not only from the difficulty which would follow a possible victory of the Turks, but also from the danger of a war in Europe which would follow if the Powers found themselves, unprepared, face to face with a Turco-Bulgarian conflict.

The course of events may be predicted. If the Sultan did not surrender to the inevitable, the only railway which connects the capital with Macedonia could be destroyed by Bulgarian dynamite at one of the many bridges and tunnels in the narrow defile near Drama, and, with transports prevented from leaving the Dardanelles, the Turkish army of the West would be cut off. Relieved of this danger, the Bulgarian army, as most military experts hold, would reach Constantinople. But before this the occupation of Smyrna or Gallipoli by the naval Powers concerned would have paralysed Turkey. It is enough to show that she cannot resist. In actual fact, she will save herself from collapse by accepting control of Macedonia by the Concert. A conference of the Powers will be called, and the scandal, which Lord Lansdowne called a menace to European peace, will have disappeared.

The ultimate result of such intervention—if the Powers did not step in, as in Crete, and assume control—might be a partition among the small States. This is no matter for alarm. It would mean that we had arrived at a permanent disposal of the problem.

The bare possibility that the small Powers would be actually paralysed by their differences, or that the pressure which the two adjacent empires could bring upon them would be adequate to prevent hostilities, does not vitiate the policy. In that event the situation would be left unchanged. Macedonia would not be in a worse plight than before, for the fear that a joint action might at any time be arranged would act as a constant incentive to the Powers to favour reform and to the Turks to accept it.

In practice, no such action is required. What, then, is suggested if certain Powers will not join in enforcing control by the Concert? It is that England should reiterate definitely the proposal made by Lord Lansdowne and Sir Edward Grey for the establishment of a Commission in Macedonia representing the Powers and having administrative and executive authority, and should undertake to carry out, as a mandatory of the Powers, the necessary naval action. This proposal should be accompanied by an intimation that under no circumstances will England take part in preventing attack by the small Powers upon Turkey for the liberation of Macedonia. To any such means as may be required to bring the question publicly before the Concert—it may be a special conference or a diplomatic mission—the Government will find universal support in this country. Publicity itself is a potent weapon, in that the Eastern Powers are unwilling to appear as the avowed enemies of reform for peoples kindred to their own.

Few would deny that, if Macedonia can be liberated without either landing an army or the risk of a European war, our obligation does extend beyond making suggestions to the Concert. If it is a matter of vigorous diplomacy and movements of the fleet alone, it is nowhere argued that we should refuse any trouble and expense that can effect reform.

It is at running the risk of war that we draw the line, and rightly draw it. The fear of war is often vaguely employed to excuse ourselves from action which, though troublesome, is perfectly safe. The line would, in reality, be clearly drawn at the point where any great Power threatens to regard our coercion of Turkey as a hostile act.

With regard to the first, the mere fact that the British fleet might sail for Smyrna was in 1880 sufficient to obtain submission, and the withdrawal of the Turkish army and government from Thessaly. At the worst, as during the demonstration of 1905, it is a matter of landing small parties to occupy custom-houses under cover of the fleet. Thus the action contemplated offers no such opportunity for an enemy to take advantage of our embarrassment as is sometimes thoughtlessly urged.

Nor should we be flying in the face of Austrian designs, for Austria has declared, in December, 1906, for a solution on lines of national autonomy if the *status quo* is disturbed. But, on the other hand, if any Power should threaten hostile resistance to such action, our course is clear. Supposing this event to come about—that European Powers should make war for the continuance of massacre—then we should be free to reply, as Mr. Gladstone suggested in 1896: "We cast upon you who are willing to undertake it the responsibility of giving countenance to these detestable proceedings. We wash our hands of them. We will do what was done by France in 1840, without loss of honour, retaining our own judgment and our right of enforcing that judgment when we see our way to it. But we will not plunge Europe into war, and will leave to those who bring about this state of things the responsibility which belongs to them. . . . I declare," he continued, "in my judgment it would be far better even to run the risk, which I believe is no risk at all, of recession, than to continue the present state of things, in which we become ministers and co-operators with . . . monstrous acts."

To-day there is no desire, as of old, to support Turkey, and we cannot complain even of unwillingness on the part of our Government to join other Powers in advocating reform; but neither can we accept the statement that everything possible has been done. The Concert needs a leader. Is England called upon to lead? Without question, we are bound to claim, she is. Other Powers are hampered in special ways, and England is responsible before all others for the scandal of Macedonia. Such is the magnitude of this scandal that few aims of policy, not even the desire to be polite to our friends, should supersede the duty to fulfil our obligations.

The Bulgarian Prime Minister during a recent conversation was urging the difficulty of restraining his country from war with Turkey, and complaining of the conduct of the Powers. When I asked what he would do himself if he were English Foreign Minister, I hardly expected the restraint and accuracy of his reply. "Well," he said, "I should push harder."

CHAPTER VI

THE REAL QUESTION

Magnitude of the evil—British responsibility—Political ethics—Waste of wealth—The use of force—The battle of rival ideals—Practical aspects—Political action for interest or duty—The need of public attention—What we can do

THERE comes to us from Macedonia an appeal which cannot be neglected. It is not a mere matter of relieving pain: it is a matter of making the barest necessities of decent life, even family morality itself, possible to great populations, and those, too, not ignorant or savage, but of the type which has made civilization.

Neither does it affect a limited number only. British slavery itself affected directly but 700,000 souls. The population of European Turkey is probably over three millions.

Nor is it a call for sympathy such as comes to us from sufferers in Russia, for over them we have no control. It is not in our power to relieve them, while the misery of Macedonia is our own creation, and its termination depends mainly on our efforts.

The question raises thoughts of a wider problem than the relief of suffering; it recalls the unity of the civilized world. Cross Europe from end to end, and though you pass through commercial barriers and hostile armies, you see in every land a type of social order which is common to all. It is a type found only in Europe and her daughter States. It is a type which makes Europe, though so small a corner of the world that you can traverse it in three days, foremost of all the continents. The spirit and the source of it are everywhere the same. Yet it is paralyzed by dissension. The conflict, when it comes, will represent the extension of order and humane ideals. The peoples of Europe share in the duty which falls on a special constable. The work must be done by force. War in such a case is the task of the policeman. If the Great Powers, who alone can perform it without resistance and bloodshed, throw the burden on small States, to whom it means untold danger and suffering, it is for the people of Europe to aid them by every means at their disposal.

Again, to know of ghastly deeds and to be conscious of the power to prevent them, and yet to sit still, must relax all morality. Here is a fatal danger to Europe. Something corresponding to the need must be done. Without a disinterested policy abroad our own prosperity has no justification.

There is a modern tendency to keep the eyes

fixed on the material aspect of empire, and for those who habitually take a bird's-eye view of the world it is difficult to realize vividly the outlook of the dwellers on a single spot. The spread of wealth and the confusion of subjects for thought, these seem to have produced a decay of feeling. The public mind has no such vigour as it displayed for Italian freedom.

We deliberately postpone the claims of nationality to arrangements of convenience. The action of Canning and Lord John Russell recognized no distinction between material and moral interests. It was based on the view that the British were a liberty-loving race, and would not stand unmoved when freedom was at stake.

Yet we admit that the pursuit of "interest" in Turkey has spelt waste of wealth and loss of historic treasure. Commerce demands that lands by nature wealthy, fields that were once the world's granary, and mines which were flourishing in Roman days should not lie idle at our very door.

What the archæologist may gain when order arrives in Turkey, Dr. Evans has shown by his discoveries in Crete. Turkey is filled with neglected stores of similar wealth.

But the most disastrous waste of all is that of vigorous peoples, suddenly checked in their growth at the very moment that they were entering, with the rest of Europe, on a period of modern development.

Like a plant placed in the dark, they remain stifled and arrested at the level of mediaeval life. Can anything be more tragic than that, when mankind through the piled-up efforts of countless generations has attained to some habits of goodwill, some general distaste for violence, these hard-won gains should be destroyed by the imposition of anarchy?

We are driven to ask ourselves, What are the social ideals that we hold worth working for? The cynic tells us that persecutor and persecuted are equally bad; small nations are a failure; they have never shown themselves able to conquer; it were better if other nations now liberated had been left to the Turk. It is well for us, then, to consider, What is of any value to our so-called civilization? What are the achievements which characterize it? Are they conquest and dominion, which belonged to Christian and Moslem alike, or are they rather the achievement of literature, of art, of freedom for men and for women, of social betterment, of political organization, mastery over material Nature? These distinguish the small Christian States equally with the great conquerors, and that which has fashioned them is at bottom the Christian maxim, "Thou shalt love thy neighbour as thyself." It was upon far other ideals that the choice of Mohammed fell.

The question arises, Is all this a matter of religion? Whether our ideals will live without it at least a hundred years will be required to prove, but that they did not grow without it is certain. One thing is clear—that the clash of East and West is a conflict of two fundamental principles of life, as expressed in material force—the Mohammedan principle of fatalism and the Christian principle of progress.

Unless to all these questions we make the reply of the cynic, they lead us to the practical field, and of necessity (because it is a matter of foreign affairs) to the principles on which a Government should act. In practice the simple instincts of self-preservation on the one hand or of humanity on the other usually point with sufficient clearness to action. But here is a case where the issue is confused and little understood; and now, more than of yore, we feel the need of theoretic principles to justify action. What is the first and simplest theory on which we ought to proceed? It is the simple principle which the Duke of Argyll enunciates in his volume on our duty to Turkey when he says: "Every Christian nation has a commission to remove such evils as may be accessible to its efforts." But this commission is overshadowed by the more obvious duty of redressing the wrongs for which we are ourselves responsible, and no obscurity clouds our sense of obligation to rescue the people whom we placed in slavery in 1878. Again, to every lover of our country and the principles for which Great Britain stands it is clearly our tradition to encourage self-government among all those who are fit for it.

It is a question less easily answered, What is the true nature of British interests? On this our relations with Turkey throw light; it makes clear that if interest is to govern our action, it should be pursued with an enlightened and liberal spirit. To obstruct Russia by supporting Turkey was a policy now regretted, both on moral and political grounds. To safeguard liberty and commerce also by promoting autonomy and national rights is a policy equally interested and just. It was adopted by Lord Salisbury and Lord Lansdowne, but with inadequate vigour. Liberation is not alone a matter of humanity. We want not less but more attention to the problem of our real interests. England is, above all, concerned in spreading the idea of legality among the nations, and disinterested conduct, if history is to be a guide, brings in the end its material reward.

A different problem is involved in the question, What duty has a Government to express the moral feeling of its nation? International politics are the last field of human action to which morals are applied; the simplest moral principle, that of the Good Samaritan, albeit enunciated by the Duke of Argyll, is not accepted as applicable to States. A minister has to consider—be his policy one of interest or humanity—whether public feeling is adequate to justify the cost or the risk. He is trustee for the public estate, and must not act on his desires alone.

But in regard to Turkey there is no lack of public desire for action, even at a monetary sacrifice; the danger is rather this—that the policy of supporting a reform is so widely accepted by Liberal and Conservative alike, that the stimulus of party feeling is lacking to push forward the question, so that a Government to-day has not so much to refrain from going beyond public support as to take care that a cause which is silent because it commands universal consent shall not be neglected.

It has sometimes been too little considered on what principles interference by the public in foreign affairs should proceed. Experience has not been fortunate. It has usually taken the shape of epidemic outbursts of public clamour, suddenly prompted by the discovery that material interest or humane duty was at stake. In a country like England the public will never be debarred from asserting itself in this way in foreign affairs; and the moral of history is not so much that laymen should leave the Foreign Office to itself as that their concern should be continuous and well-informed, in order that it may never be panic-stricken. The Turkish Question, being remote and complicated and not often in the public mind, requires above all others specially assiduous concern. Other questions have competed with it at the very time that it most needed attention. When it became practical, in 1903, Mr. Chamberlain had just launched the cause of Protection; then came the Russo-Japanese war, and afterwards the Russian revolution. From dragging its course so long, and from the knowledge that in the past it has involved us in huge mistakes, the question has become wearisome. The facts of the case are so disgusting that no one likes to speak of them; they are so revolting that while in a way we believe them we do not visually accept the belief. Although we admit the responsibility, yet the Turkish Question is one which we would most gladly ignore, because our interference has been disastrous in the past.

It is to meet the needs of those who feel these difficulties that permanent organizations are required.[1]

The public conscience demands expression when it is aggrieved. But, above all, we must concern ourselves with action; no generous impulse of ours must deter us from this guiding principle. If no reform can result from agitation, agitators must keep quiet. For this reason, above all, the attention of experts is needed, so that the time for action may be rightly chosen, and false hopes among the oppressed, which might lead, as they have sometimes done, to further sufferings, may not be raised. An expert organization should ascertain what are the possibilities of the diplomatic situation. Satisfied on this point, what it can do is to provide a support to the Foreign Minister, and an argument, based on

[1] *Vide* Appendix, "The Balkan Committee."

the fact that public opinion demands activity, which the Government can use in urging action upon other Powers. Lord Salisbury and Lord Lansdowne made use of this argument in a number of cases. By supporting such a committee, every one can do something for the cause, whether by financial aid or by arousing interest in others. Government, however remote from direct criticism, is the reflection of public opinion and in the end obeys the public will; influence is increased by organization and it is by joining in exerting influence that every one in this case can do some tangible thing to make possible a life of decency in a hundred thousand homes.

We neglect the claim of those who suffer for our mistaken action at our peril. Nations, equally with persons, must pay dearly for neglect of duty. It is by the clearest duty that we are bound to make the utmost of every opportunity. It is by the call of common human nature to aid the victim of cruelty; by the proud tradition of our country, chiefly famous for promoting liberty and national right; by the simple debt of honour, incurred through our action in the past, and not yet paid.

CHAPTER VII

WHAT A TRAVELLER SEES

The free States—Mediaeval colouring—Monasteries—The Turkish frontier—Austrian humour—The tragedy

THREE days' travelling will take one out of Europe and into "the East," while a six-weeks holiday permits of a visit to Albania, a country almost as wild as Afghanistan. It is a rare opportunity, this relic of the Middle Ages, brought to our doors by the Orient express; and it cannot last, for civilization creeps on. Yet those who seize the fleeting privilege may be counted on the fingers.

The maps of the schoolroom teach us to include the Balkan Peninsula in Europe, but, once across the Danubian plains, the traveller will not be long before he discovers himself to be in another zone. He has passed at once into a mediaeval world: gorgeous national dress confronts him at every village; the dingy garb of the West has given way to the flowing robe of the Mohammedan Mullah and the long hair of the Orthodox priest.

The free States of the Balkans combine the charms of East and West. Where Westernism is creeping in it adds to the humour, if not the beauty, of the scene. These nations—Bulgaria, Greece, Montenegro, Servia, and Roumania—once in the front of civilization, long enslaved and now set free, play with their new Constitutions like children with a toy, and with a similar result—the toy gets broken. On my first visit to Belgrade I made the acquaintance of two members of the Ministry; on my next visit I was hoping to meet them, but was laughed at for my simplicity: they had gone where ministers naturally go—one was in prison, the other in exile.

But the humours of politics are only the bubbles on the surface; there is a deep current of happiness and prosperity, following on the release from bondage. The ancient monasteries, always the symbol of national hopes, but often robbed and ruined in the days of the captivity, are now the scene of such festive happiness as the West knows no longer. At Studenitsa 10,000 people gather to celebrate the Virgin's birthday. At Rilo 7,000 pilgrims sleep in the galleries and the 500 rooms of the monastery itself. They are all the guests of the abbot, whose cook, with his wooden spoon, 6 feet long, serves out dinners from the monastic cooking-pot, a fixed vessel large enough to contain two oxen together.

Religious festivals, as formerly in the West, are the occasion of commercial fairs; the fair, again, attracts the whole race of mirth-providers. Dancing occupies the evening, and here may still be seen the blind minstrels of Homeric type, singing of national glories long passed, to the strains of the one-stringed guitar. Neither is religion forgotten. At 5 a.m. the monks begin to say Mass, and at daybreak I have hardly found standing-room in the chapel. Round its colonnade are pictures showing the sufferings of the wicked in another world: those of brigands seem to attract most attention, and the abbot will tell you that these need no apology—it is the only way to teach the illiterate peasant. Life here seems very far from the Western world; and when one learns that in this chapel was held a memorial service at Mr. Gladstone's death, one feels surprised that they have ever heard of him.

Round the village there is often a large common, covered in autumn with broad sheets of the purple crocus. Here grazes the village herd of dun-coloured cattle, each beast finding its own way in the evening to its master's house in the village street. In this meadow on Sunday afternoon the village gathers for the *horo*, the national dance. A circle of dancers forms round the fiddler (or, if they be Bulgarians, the piper), and whether the number in the circle be six or a hundred, no Western party could compete with it for vigorous mirth. In Bulgaria, while the dancing is going on, you may meet the school-children, led by the schoolmaster, who is compelled by official order to take his pupils on Sunday afternoon for a natural-history ramble.

For the politician, too, there are cheering sights. If he reflects sadly on the puzzles of religious education, he will be cheered by the splendid achievement of the Austrian Government in Bosnia. Thirty years ago Moslem, Roman Catholic, and Greek Catholic lived in perpetual and bloodstained feud; now their children sit together in the school. The rival clerics collect their followers in different rooms during the hour for religious teaching (content that the "atmosphere" should at other times be merely patriotic), and then the rival sectarians, so lately at war, gather again for playtime in the school-yard.

In these liberated countries the tourist may travel with perfect safety. The Government will, indeed, offer him a gendarme for escort, and he will be well advised to take him, but not to ward off brigands; there is more danger from fierce dogs (such as killed, in this very land, the great Euripides), and these the escort is instructed, if necessary, to shoot; or if the traveller arrives benighted at some village where the inn appears abnormally verminous, the gendarme will justify his pay by demanding the hospitality of the best house in the village. Brigandage need not distress the traveller outside Turkey, though I plead guilty to fear on one occasion in Bulgaria. It was just after the capture by Bulgarian brigands in Turkey of an American lady missionary. She was, indeed, reported to be concealed in the very monastery to which we were travelling. The district hourly expected the brigands to appear, for a Bulgarian paper of the district had reported that my friend and I were setting out to ransom the lady, carrying £25,000 in our pockets. Considering the temptation, it does indeed speak well for the Bulgarian Government that no violent hands were laid upon us.

The dominions of the Sultan have their charms also for holiday-making; the mountains are beautiful, the tattered escort is picturesque, and barbarism is often funny. On first setting out for the Balkans I told the then Turkish Ambassador in London that I was going in search of health, and in particular for a weak throat; the Ambassador quaintly replied, "It is not a very good place for throats." That is no doubt the case for the subjects of the Sultan, but for the European traveller it is safe enough: and, whether it be from the mountain air or from the total absence of luxury, those who have tried the Balkans have always found them exhilarating.

The Turkish frontier is always alarming. It is not, like most frontiers, an unreal and shadowy existence. The passage from one world to another is immediately signalized by the mouldering customhouse and the tattered uniform. Usually as civilization increases the picturesque disappears, but here it is not so. "Where the Turkish foot treads the grass never grows." When the Turk is gone, houses are rebuilt and roads are made, but nothing beautiful is destroyed, for there was none to destroy, except the minarets, which usually remain. The new eaves are wider and the roads shadier, and orchards relieve the brown monotony of the Turkish waste. Entering Turkey, you leave both prosperity and beauty at once. The poverty of some parts is extreme. When I entered Turkey from Servia, the Governor sent a message begging me to bring carriages from Servia if I wanted them, as there were none available in his country.

But to return to the frontier. There is a glorious uncertainty about what will happen. One man is turned back and has his journey nipped in the bud; another is arrested on the suspicion of being an agitator; at the best every item of his luggage is strewn on the floor, and his books, when the official has pretended to read them, usually holding them upside down, are taken from him. On one occasion, by way of experiment, we took with us a copy of the Koran and an anti-Turkish pamphlet; the Turk returned to us the pamphlet, but declined to pass the Koran—his own national Bible. After this we became friendly, and he expressed regret that he could not allow us to take the Koran; but, reflecting that we might reward him with a bribe, he added that if we would go back into Bosnia and post the book from there to our destination in Turkey, he would allow it to pass, as he was not ordered to examine the post. This was done, and the Sultan's commands thus duly obeyed.

In Turkey there is not much pleasure to be derived from the contemplation of happiness or of natural beauty, except where Nature has been left untouched; but there is humour, though the humour generally brings its inconveniences. A bear-hunting party in the mountains was decidedly quaint. Our host, the manager of a mine in which the villagers worked, entertained us in a battlemented castle, from which he never stirred without a rifle. He began by giving orders that every villager should be ready at 4 a.m. to go out and beat the forest, or he would himself be beaten with the birch. Arrived at the shooting-ground, he posted us for the drive, and gave us strict orders, if we saw any man whom we did not know to be one of the beaters, to shoot him without delay; it was best to run no risks. We demurred to the chance of shooting an honest peasant, but this, he said, mattered nothing; the mayor of the village himself would at the most cost £20. When we finally left the village, he implored us not to let our intentions be known, because we should certainly be kidnapped; and he proceeded, as a measure of precaution, to order all the villagers to the forest in another direction for an imaginary bear-hunt. Having thus put brigands off the scent, he got up at three o'clock in the morning and saw us off.

One of the strangest things in Turkey is the contempt with which the Turks are treated by some of their Moslem subjects. At Novibazar, in "old Servia," Albanians amused themselves by jostling the Turkish Prefect as he was showing us the town. These men wear ragged white clothes and have their heads shaven, except for a long tag of hair at the back, which gives them an amazingly savage appearance; they all carry rifles, even the boys, as soon as they can bear the weight of a Martini. When I was at Mitrovitza, they had recently broken open the prison and driven away the Turkish troops; in 1903 they expelled the representative of the Russian Empire. A dense crowd of them were gathered at our departure from Novibazar, to demonstrate their hostility to the suspected stranger. The impotence of their so-called Turkish Governor was comical to witness, but I must confess to considerable anxiety to be out of the crowd. At Prishtina they had murdered the Servian Consul, and the buildings of the tobacco monopoly, which the Turks had attempted to establish, had served to provide them with a bonfire. A certain Suliman Pasha, an Albanian of that place, quite overshadowed the Turkish Governor. He was celebrating his daughter's wedding, at which 3,000 of his Albanian compatriots attended with their rifles. The feasting was going on for a week, and we were invited to one of the banquets. A Turkish dinner, where you have to sit on the floor, tear up roast ducks with your hands, and appropriate innumerable courses without intermission, is always a painful trial. If you stop for an instant, your host will avenge himself by forcing upon you an even larger portion. Your sufferings are vastly increased by having to sit cramped upon the floor. Besides, at a real Turkish meal only one glass is provided, and a servant, who carries it with a jug of water, brings it to the guest who wishes to drink; the terrible choice has, therefore, to be made between eating ten large courses without any drink and the unspeakable qualms of sharing the vessel with your companions.

The solemnity of calling on a Turk, with its inevitable programme of coffee, cigarette, and jam with water, its slow repetition of hypocritical compliments and renewed cigarettes, is amusing to a beginner. It was especially so at Plevlis, where the Austrians had till 1909 a garrison in Turkish territory. The Austrian General took us to the Pasha, and discoursed, as is customary, on the excellent roads and bridges which the Pasha had built. I supposed that, as usual, there were no roads; but I had not realized the pungency of

Austrian wit. We learnt afterwards that there was a road and even a bridge, but both had been built by the Austrian himself. I remember coming once on a very fine bridge, an astonishing and welcome sight. The bridge was not Turkish, but Byzantine; it would have been, however, none the less welcome, but that the river had changed its course, and no longer ran under the Roman bridge —or any other.

Austrian humour went to even greater lengths of savagery: on the bare limestone hills surrounding Plevlis they had written in huge letters of white stones the monogram of the Austrian Kaiser, and they discoursed to the Turks of the charming effect produced when these emblems (humiliating to Turkey) were illuminated on the Kaiser's birthday.

If the company of a Mohammedan becomes oppressive, you can generally remove him by producing some article condemned by Mohammed, such as ham or bacon; but the old piety is breaking down, and the decay of fanaticism synchronises with the growing popularity of the bottle. My friend and I engaged a Mohammedan dragoman, and started out with him the first day with a modest lunch, chiefly of ham and whisky, with some suitable viands for the true believer. We produced the ham bashfully, out of regard for his feelings; but, to our disgust, he displayed a liking for ham equalling our own, with an appetite twice as voracious. He explained that, though a Turk, he was a Liberal. We afterwards crossed the boundary into Montenegro (where a Turk might be unpopular), and found, to our astonishment, that our friend had become a Christian, having hidden his fez and produced an English cap from his pocket. After this he changed his religion no less than three times, avoiding awkward consequences with great skill, except once when he found it convenient to join with us in declaring himself a Protestant, with the result that he was completely cornered by an inquisitive Greek monk, who demanded to know the Protestant view of the Virgin Mary.

The humours of travel, however, are not to be obtained without a corresponding share of discomfort. A Turkish inn is frequently little more than a range of rotten shanties surrounding a manure-heap, so that the traveller will probably choose a room looking on to the open street, and get as near to the open window as he can. At one place, however, we were not allowed even this luxury; the officer of the escort politely requested us to keep at the other end of the room, and proceeded to draw some curtains across the windows, explaining that the Albanians resented the presence of foreign travellers, and might take the opportunity of shooting them from the street through the window. On leaving the room I fell over the prostrate form of one of the escort; they had had orders not to let us leave their sight, and being sleepy, he had stretched himself across the door. At another place we were very anxious to learn the opinions of a Christian merchant; the problem was how to shake off the escort. It was impossible to do so ourselves, so we agreed to go for a walk in the town (which would compel the escort to go with us), and to leave our interpreter for a talk with the merchant, which he might afterwards report to us. But the Christians implored us to desist; it was as much as their liberty was worth even to be seen talking to the interpreter. Their fears were not ungrounded: two days after we had left the place, and were staying with the Servian Consul elsewhere, a message reached him that a schoolmaster who had been speaking to our servant (albeit in the presence of the escort) had been arrested and thrown into prison. A suspicious escort is a scourge. Only on one occasion did we rid ourselves of it. We were spending the night at a small mountain farm, and the farmer had shown his appreciation by killing one of his herd of swine, which he roasted whole for our benefit over a wood fire. The captain of the escort was, fortunately, a pious Moslem, and when the pig was brought in he fled, and we found ourselves for the first time left alone with the Christians. The Servian Consul, who was with us, and who would have means of verifying statements, seized the opportunity of asking the farmer how things were going on. He replied that the Albanians had demanded from him a ransom of £30, and that, as he could not possibly pay, he would be obliged to fly across the frontier into Servia, abandoning all his property; he wanted advice from the Consul as to how he was to provide for his wife, his mother, and his children. He added that his father and his uncle had been murdered by Albanians. The Consul then inquired, by way of verification, where the murder had taken place. The farmer immediately answered, "It was in this room," and then pointed out two bullet-holes in the wall.

The Turkish drama is indeed more distinguished for tragedy than comedy. The Servian Bishop at Uskub was very anxious to hear about the English stage, and added: "Here we have no theatre, but we are noted for our tragedies." The statement was confirmed by an incident which took place a few days before. A Bulgarian girl had been stolen by a Turk, and her brother begged the Russian Consul to give her shelter if she was rescued. The Consul was so far satisfied of the facts that he did so, and sent the girl with his wife to Bulgaria. Soon afterwards the brother was found with his throat cut, close to the Turk's house. Several Christians (but not the Turk) were thereupon arrested, and there, as usual, things ended. It is not to be wondered at that the daughters of Christians, as well as of Turks, are hidden under the veil in many districts after they are ten years old. A friend of ours was appealed to by

INDUSTRIAL WASTE : A BURNT FARM

a Christian woman in our presence for advice, because the village gendarme had expelled her husband and taken her into his house, and had now gone away, leaving her in trouble and unprovided for. At another village the schoolmaster replied to our inquiries that all was quiet, they were very happy; but when asked for details, he said that the Turkish sergeant had closed the inn every evening because the innkeeper's wife had refused his advances, but he had not thought such things worth mentioning. He added that he had also been beaten himself, but he did not know why. I was reminded of an Armenian guide at Constantinople, who said that he had not suffered by the massacres. When I asked him if none of his relations had been killed, he replied: "Yes, one of my brothers was killed, but only one."

The most tragic situation exists in parts of Albania where the Albanian population is mixed with the Macedonian or (as in "old Servia") the Servian. Here, in addition to the hardships of Turkish government, the defenceless Christians are at the mercy of a savage race, more active than the Turks, forming in practice a class of licensed brigands, respecting no authority, and living by raids on Christian villages. In Abul Hamid's time the Governor of this district, though strongly anti-Christian, made some attempt to keep the Albanians in order. The Sultan had an Albanian guard, and his personal safety demanded that the

Albanians should be humoured, so the unhappy Governor was transferred to Tripoli, whither his secretary had preceded him, having made himself suspected of treasonable radicalism by importing a bicycle. In the same part of Albania I was breakfasting one day with one of the Consuls, when a dishevelled and miserable Servian monk arrived. He had been in charge of a monastery. Some Albanians had arrived, plundered the monastery, and promised him a bullet if he did not go. The great monastery of Detchane, one of the historic and sacred memorials of the Servian Empire, has often been plundered by tribes over whom Turkish authority is absolutely nil. I have even seen an aged priest who was driven to carry a revolver and a Martini rifle himself, so often had he been attacked; he was anxious to explain that for this irregularity he had a licence from the Bishop. It was specially welcome at that time, because war was raging between the Turkish authority and the Albanian chief, Isa Bolietinatz. Isa objected to the establishment of a Russian Consulate, and compelled the Turks to refuse the Russian demand. I visited this gentleman's castle. It was a lofty stone building, with walls three feet thick, an iron door, windows with stone shutters, and loopholes for rifles on every side. The strangest part of this establishment is a small monastery, which, though a Mohammedan, he has founded close to the castle, and in which he keeps an unfortunate monk of the Greek Church practically a prisoner, compelling him to do his bidding on a starvation wage.

Such are some of the chance incidents of a traveller's holiday. It is amazing that signs of violence should be visible to him. A traveller is so far removed from the realities of local life that any trouble he may actually see is as the far-driven smoke which proves a great fire.

APPENDICES

A—BERLIN TREATY, 1878

Article XXIII

"The Sublime Porte undertakes scrupulously to apply in the Island of Crete the Organic Law of 1868, with such modifications as may be considered equitable.

"Similar laws adapted to local requirements, excepting as regards the exemption from taxation granted to Crete, shall also be introduced into the other parts of Turkey in Europe, for which no special organization has been provided by the present Treaty.

"The Sublime Porte shall depute Special Commissions, in which the native element shall be largely represented, to settle the details of the new laws in each province.

"The schemes of organization resulting from these labours shall be submitted for examination to the Sublime Porte, which, before promulgating the Acts for putting them into force, shall consult the European Commission instituted for Eastern Roumelia."

Article LXII (Extract)

"In no part of the Ottoman Empire shall difference of religion be alleged against any person as a ground for exclusion or incapacity as regards the discharge of civil and political rights, admission to the public employments, functions, and honours, or the exercise of the various professions and industries.

"All persons shall be admitted, without distinction of religion, to give evidence before the tribunals.'

B—LORD LANSDOWNE'S PROPOSAL TO THE FRENCH GOVERNMENT, JANUARY, 1905

His Majesty's Government suggest that the Powers should now demand—

(*a*) An immediate reduction of the military forces now maintained by Turkey in Macedonia and its neighbourhood to the number strictly required for the maintenance of internal order and security! this number to be fixed for a definite period of years. It would be reasonable to expect that Bulgaria would, in this event, be willing to carry out a simultaneous and corresponding reduction.

(*b*) The appointment for a term of years of a Commission consisting of delegates nominated by the Powers, and placed under the presidency of the Inspector-General.

The commission would be given administrative and executive powers, and would, in the first instance, be instructed to frame, without delay, schemes for the effective control of the administration of finance and justice. The financial reforms should include commutation of the tithes and provide for a fixed payment to the Porte by each of the Macedonian vilayets, the balance of the revenue collected remaining available for local purposes. The Inspector-General, assisted by the Commission, might be entrusted with the command of such Turkish troops as it might be found necessary to retain in Macedonia.

C—THE BALKAN COMMITTEE

President

Professor Westlake, K.C., Regius Professor of International Law in the University of Cambridge.

Vice-Presidents

The Earl of Aberdeen.
Rev. Canon Barnett.
Right Rev. The Bishop of Birmingham.
Lord Brassey.
George Cadbury.
Lady Frederick Cavendish.
Rev. Dr. Clifford.
Lord Gladstone.
Rev. Canon Scott Holland.
Right Rev. The Bishop of Hereford.
Right Rev. The Bishop of Lichfield.
Right Rev. The Bishop of Liverpool.
Rev. F. B. Meyer.
Professor Miliukoff.
Lord Stanmore.

Hon. Treasurer

R. A. Yerburgh, M.P.

General Committee

Godfrey Benson.
Rev. Rosslyn Bruce.
G. K. Chesterton.
Hon. C. F. Collier.
Professor R. S. Conway.
Rev. Percy Dearmer.
Lord Farrer.
Rev. T. C. Fry, D.D.
Professor Rendel Harris.
Professor Jenks.
F. W. Pethick Lawrence.
The Earl of Lytton.
J. M. Macdonald, M.P.
Miss Josephine Marshall.
D. M. Mason, M.P.
Edward McCurdy.
Rev. Henry Bickersteth Ottley.
Rev. Canon Rawnsley.
Miss Richardson.
Rt. Hon. Sir Albert Spicer, Bart., M.P.
Right Rev. The Bishop of Stepney.
Arthur G. Symonds, M.A.
F. G. Thomas.
C. P. Trevelyan, M.P.
G. M. Trevelyan.
L. Villari.

Executive Committee

Chairman.—Noel Buxton, M.P.

E. Gurney Boyle.
H. N. Brailsford.
E. W. Brooks.
Charles Roden Buxton.
Bertram Christian.
W. M. Crook.
Arthur Evans, F.R.S.
A. G. Gardiner.
G. P. Gooch.
J. L. Hammond.
Cecil Harris.
C. E. Hecht.
L. T. Hobhouse.
Hugh Law, M.P.
Hon. J. C. Lyttelton, M.P.
G. R. Malloch.
C. F. G. Masterman, M.P.
Rev. Canon J. H. B. Masterman.
H. W. Nevinson.
T. P. Newbould.
A. M. Scott, M.P.
R. A. Scott-James.
Alfred Stead.
H. J. Torr.
Aneurin Williams.
Hilton Young.
J. Howard Whitehouse M.P.
P. W. Wilson.

HON. SECRETARY

Sir E. Boyle, Bart.

SECRETARY

Arthur G. Symonds, M.A.

Office: 41, Tothill Street, Westminster, S.W.

BANKERS

Robartes, Lubbock & Co., 15, Lombard Street, E.C.

The objects of the Committee may be stated as follows:

1. To educate public opinion in the knowledge that grave responsibilities were incurred by Great Britain in 1878 through the Treaty of Berlin, when she secured the restoration of Macedonia to the rule of the Turk.

Had it not been for English action in 1878, the whole of the area of massacre and outrage in 1903 would have been part of a free and prosperous Balkan State.

2. To focus public opinion by the organization of meetings, and the publication of accurate news as to the state of the country. Lord Lansdowne, in 1903, appealed for expressions of public opinion in order to strengthen his hands.

3. By means of the Press, Parliament, and direct communication with the Foreign Office, to keep before His Majesty's Government what we believe to be the inflexible attitude of informed English opinion as to the Macedonian question.

4. To co-operate with the movement for Macedonian reform in France, Italy, Germany, the United States, Russia and Austria, so as to secure, as far as possible, common aims and action.

5. To promote the interests of all the Balkan States in this country, and to encourage travel in those countries and a sympathetic study of their history, customs, and institutions. It is the Committee's hope that these States may be allowed to develop their own national life and institutions free from foreign interference.

6. *To keep always in the forefront, as the firm conviction oj this country and the essential claim of its policy, the statement that no reforms are worth the paper they are written on unless they provide for the transference of executive control trom the hands of the Sultan to those of European officials; and further, that unless some such reform is very speedily carried out bloodshed and anarchy in Macedonia will find their climax in a war, which may possibly lead to a European conflagration, and certainly affords a prospect to avert which a most determined effort should be made on the part of all lovers of peace.*

D—A TURKISH PRISON

THE prisons are not only crowded so full that the prisoners cannot lie down at night, but torture is common; and merely to extort statements which may incriminate others, whether false or true, unthinkable sufferings are inflicted. The following is, perhaps, a piece of evidence worth repeating, because it is seldom that ocular evidence is available. It is confirmed in this case beyond any shadow of doubt.

It is part of a recent letter from a European deserving of every confidence. The names of the persons tortured, places, as well as the dates, are suppressed, for fear that the Turkish officials should take revenge on the injured persons. There are details in the letter which are quite unfit for publication:

"Five of the men imprisoned here have been released and have returned, nothing being found against them. I have taken the statements of three of these from their own mouths, and give them below.

"One of these men says that he was taken to prison and was to have been put into the common prison with the criminals; but found a corporal who was a friend of his, who secured the privilege for him of being sent to the barracks instead, and that no indignities were practised on him. He was examined and nothing found against him, and he was released. Of course he had to provide his own bedding and food, and fee his gaolers freely; but that is a matter of course, and is hardly counted as a cause of complaint.

"Another man, one of the prominent and well-to-do men in the community, was arrested and thrown into prison just before nightfall. He was put into a room in the criminals' prison, where fourteen condemned criminals were serving out sentences for varying terms, some even for life as murderers. He was stripped naked, was made to kneel on a stick of rough firewood with another stick behind his knees, and thus sit on his feet; then in that position with another similar stick he was beaten on the thighs above the knees. If he leaned forward at all to relieve the strain, as he must involuntarily do, he was struck violently under the chin to force him to hold his head erect. For five days thereafter he was unable to shut his teeth together. Then he was beaten on the lower legs over the shinbones. A shoemaker's awl was driven under the nail of the third finger of the right hand, of the big toe and second toe of the right foot, and of the big toe of the left foot. There was a hole in the wall like a stovepipe hole. His hand was thrust through, and the criminals in the next room burned his hand with heated tongs in several places. Then the fire-shovel was heated in the coals, and he was burned in four places on the buttocks and back. Then with the red-hot tongs a form of torture which cannot be described was practised. Slighter burns were made on his face and forehead. His ears were pulled and twisted until they bled. Then he was compelled to drink urine (not his own) from the vessel in the room. He thanked God that the fire in the mangal was so nearly out that they could not heat the shovel again. They tried to get some fire from the next room, but it was out there also. After this he was left standing naked for at least five hours, until towards morning he was allowed to dress and sit down on the mud floor. During these tortures he was continually asked to 'confess,' to say something about some one, that such a man in the place was a member of a 'committee,' or something of that sort. But he remained firm all through. He was asked if he was a Giaour or a Mussulman, implying that if he would acknowledge Islam he would be released.

"I asked this man if he knew what other prisoners had suffered, and he said that he did not, because all were treated separately, only he heard one whom he knew screaming for mercy. Also another, who was in the next room, had his arm thrust through the same hole in the wall already mentioned, and the criminals on this side burned it, and he heard him say, 'You were the head of our committee of twenty-five,' and then added, 'I am not saying this; they are making me say it.'

"The next morning, supported by two men, he was taken before the Mutessarif, and immediately made complaint of the way in which he had been treated. He insisted on opening his clothes and showing his wounds. The Governor professed sorrow, said it was a mistake, and should not happen again. He was examined and sent back to another part of the prison, where he could be more comfortable. A physician was allowed to see him once and treat him. The city physician, a Turk, was sent to see him, but he refused treatment from him, and demanded a report from him of his condition that he might bring an action against the Government. Influential men worked for him, and finally he was sent home.

"I saw him sixteen days after the receipt of the injuries. The burns on his face were healed. The left ear was swollen and inflamed. Discoloration on upper part of the left arm from bruises was about 2 by 4 inches in extent. Third finger of right hand was much swollen, inflamed, skin peeling off, evidently in course of healing after a severe wound infection. Third finger of left hand had a large partially-healed wound, and there were seven or eight scars of burns on the back of the hand. There were four wounds on the back and buttocks, evidently from burning, not yet healed, with scabs over them, about 3 or 4 inches wide by 5 inches long. The worst wound was still red and inflamed. On each leg above the knee the discoloration from bruising was marked, extending 6 or 8 inches above the kneecap. Below the knee and on the heels were scars of bruises and burns.

"Another man arrested at the same time as those named was taken to a room next to them. He was stripped naked. His right hand and arm were thrust through the hole in the wall into the next room and burned with the tongs. An awl was thrust under the nail of the thumb. His fingers were bent back until they seemed to break. He was beaten on the back, and told to charge one of the others with being the head of the committee. He called out to him, 'Were you not the head of our committee? I am not saying this; they are compelling me to say it.' (These two men had not seen each other at all since that time, but their story agreed.) Then he was beaten more for saying this. He was placed in the same position as the first man mentioned, with the sticks under and behind the knees, and beaten on the legs above the knees with a stick of firewood. He was seized by the throat and choked. Awls were driven into the soles of his feet. A stake was sharpened and he was made to sit on it with it pressing against the perinæum, and then a man sprang on his back. The stake did not penetrate. A rope was put round his neck and drawn up until he was choking, when the "guardian" of the prison came along and told them not to do that. Later, a handkerchief was tied round his neck and twisted until he was choking, and meanwhile he was beaten on the back, but at the eighth blow he fainted. Later, long nails were brought to drive through his feet to the floor, but this was not done. He was made to stand in cold water up to the knees (still naked), holding a mangal of hot coals in his hands for an hour and a half. At the least sign of dropping it he was beaten. Some time after midnight he was allowed to crawl into the charcoal-bin and go to sleep. While still sleeping, suddenly someone took a handful of earth and crowded it into his mouth, dragged his fez down over it with one hand and choked him by the neck with the other. He seemed to be just dying when someone else released him. Blows on the head and face, small burns on the face, kicks, etc., were common all through the time, and he said he did not count that. In the morning he was brought before the Governor, and when he complained of his treatment, the Governor said, 'My son, this is a mistake. I am very sorry for it; it won't happen again.' The rest of the time he was imprisoned elsewhere. He was subsequently released. Release, of course, means that absolutely nothing was found against them.

"I saw this man on March 22, sixteen days after the receipt of the injuries. There was a large unhealed sore with a scab on his right arm, 3 inches long. The wound made by the awl is still to be seen under the nail of the right thumb, down to the root of the nail. There were three sores on the lower part of the back and buttocks in the shape of a rude cross, 4 or 5 inches each way. The men had said while doing it: 'This is your God; we will mark you with it.' There was discoloration from bruises on both legs, extending 6 inches above the knees, and on the heels. He says that one foot is still without any sensation."

. . . . .

The illness of a single friend easily engrosses all our concern. If he were the victim of torture we should be furious. If his murderer were a foreign invader, and no redress were possible, we should plan some desperate revenge. Yet, when we know of such enormities, not singly, but in hundreds, imagination fails, and we are unmoved; therefore, I make no apology for the publication of harrowing details. Without them it is quite impossible to see the facts in their true light. These things are happening to-day, and will happen till we realize them.

The Gresham Press,
UNWIN BROTHERS, LIMITED,
WOKING AND LONDON.